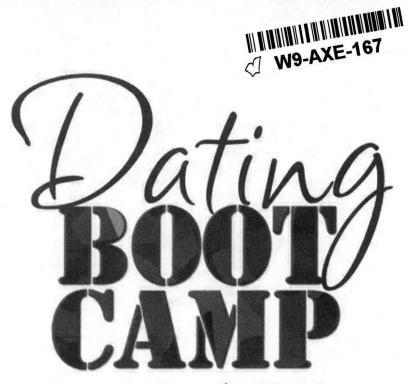

Dating BOOT CAMP

Conquering the Dating Obstacle Course

Lisa Altalida

ALPHA

A member of Penguin Group (USA) Inc.

ALPHA BOOKS

Published by the Penguin Group

Penguin Group (USA) Inc., 375 Hudson Street, New York, New York 10014, U.S.A.

Penguin Group (Canada), 10 Alcorn Avenue, Toronto, Ontario, Canada M4V 3B2 (a division of Pearson Penguin Canada Inc.)

Penguin Books Ltd, 80 Strand, London WC2R 0RL, England

Penguin Ireland, 25 St Stephen's Green, Dublin 2, Ireland (a division of Penguin Books Ltd)

Penguin Group (Australia), 250 Camberwell Road, Camberwell, Victoria 3124, Australia (a division of Pearson Australia Group Pty Ltd)

Penguin Books India Pvt Ltd, 11 Community Centre, Panchsheel Park, New Delhi—110 017, India

Penguin Group (NZ), cnr Airborne and Rosedale Roads, Albany, Auckland 1310, New Zealand (a division of Pearson New Zealand Ltd)

Penguin Books (South Africa) (Pty) Ltd, 24 Sturdee Avenue, Rosebank, Johannesburg 2196, South Africa

Penguin Books Ltd, Registered Offices: 80 Strand, London WC2R 0RL, England

International Standard Book Number: 1-59257-342-8
Library of Congress Catalog Card Number: 2004115063

06   05   04   8   7   6   5   4   3   2   1

Interpretation of the printing code: The rightmost number of the first series of numbers is the year of the book's printing; the rightmost number of the second series of numbers is the number of the book's printing. For example, a printing code of 04-1 shows that the first printing occurred in 2004.

Printed in the United States of America

Note: This publication contains the opinions and ideas of its author. It is intended to provide helpful and informative material on the subject matter covered. It is sold with the understanding that the author and publisher are not engaged in rendering professional services in the book. If the reader requires personal assistance or advice, a competent professional should be consulted.

The author and publisher specifically disclaim any responsibility for any liability, loss, or risk, personal or otherwise, which is incurred as a consequence, directly or indirectly, of the use and application of any of the contents of this book.

Most Alpha books are available at special quantity discounts for bulk purchases for sales promotions, premiums, fund-raising, or educational use. Special books, or book excerpts, can also be created to fit specific needs.

For details, write: Special Markets, Alpha Books, 375 Hudson Street, New York, NY 10014.

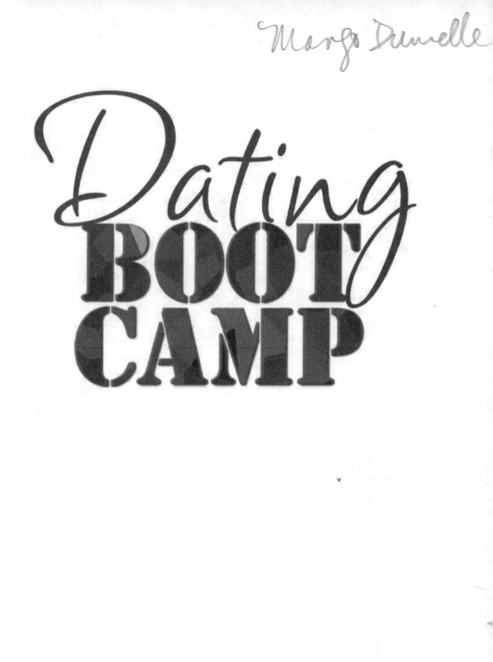

Dating BOOT CAMP

Dedicated to all of my
fellow sisters in the world:
You will find your
rainbow.

Contents

Appendix

Introduction

A lot of people have asked me, "Why did you write this book?" The answer is simple: Because I've been there and I feel your pain. It's alarming to me that the most strong, capable, beautiful, and delightful women turn into insecure, uncertain, shrinking violets when they're asked why they don't have a significant other.

Having a man joined to you at the hip doesn't define who you are! *You* define who you are. The man is just a nice complement. My life changed dramatically when I made this realization. It wasn't until I embraced my single lifestyle that I began to have more fun and enjoy more of my life, and then, finally, I found someone who was the perfect complement for me.

Women need to feel empowered.

My mission is to reach as many women as I can and remind them that they are wonderful with or without a man. Don't let your level of happiness be dictated by the social fixtures you have in your life. *You* decide what creates your happiness. By taking your power back, living your life, doing things that you enjoy, and not defining yourself by the presence or absence of a man on your arm, you will laugh more, cry less, and be more empowered to find exactly what you are looking for.

Women need to feel better about themselves.

Looks aren't everything, but in our society, they are measured pretty harshly. Regardless of what you do or don't want to change on your body, the first person that you have to please is you. If you're happy with how you look, then don't change a thing. If making a slight change to your appearance would make you feel like a starlet, then make it happen. The crime is crying about it everyday and not doing anything about it. Change can affect your life. Whether you change yourself physically or just how you look at things, do what you need to do to feel good about you.

Women need to stop feeling like it's the end of the world to be single.

Life is funny. When a woman is single, it's the biggest tragedy of all time. When a man is single, it's all about the options. Women really need to think more like men. The more opportunities you have to date, the more chances you'll have to find exactly what you're looking for.

Take a moment and think about your girlfriends who jumped at their first chance to get married. How many of these friends are divorced? Contrary to popular belief, getting married is not the goal you should be shooting for. Getting married or having a long-term commitment *with the right person* is the real goal. The more you take advantage of being single and enjoying the freedom that comes with having more options to choose from, the better your chances will be of meeting the perfect person for you.

Women can get what they want.

If you take the time and really read *Dating Boot Camp* carefully, you'll see that taking ownership of your life will make things happen. Take a hard look at the areas of your life you want to improve. Change things that you want to change. Stand up for what you believe in, and you will get what you want. The silver bullet is you: You are the one who will get you what you want.

After years of not getting what I wanted, I put myself through my own Dating Boot Camp. I began to enjoy my single lifestyle, and when it was the right time, I got what I'd always wanted. I hope that by sharing my thoughts and experiences, you, too, will stop feeling bad about what's not in your life, and instead start focusing on the possibilities. Good luck, and enjoy your *Dating Boot Camp* journey!

Acknowledgments

I give special honor to God who makes everything possible. Thank you to the special man in my life: your continued faith, love, and creative energy balance me. Many thanks to my family, friends, and *Dating Boot Camp* supporters who always keep me going. To the many women I have met on this journey who keep me inspired, thank you for your numerous questions, for which I hope to continue to have answers. To my mentor, Dr. Joy Spaulding, and my confidante, Rev. Scuzscon Walker, thank you for keeping me on the path to my dreams.

Part 1

Welcome to BOOT CAMP

Getting Ready for Boot Camp

Dating can be hard; relationships can be harder. Maybe you've realized you're tired of all the fighting. In modern armies, recruits go through a rigorous training program before they're declared soldiers—it's called boot camp. If you feel like your dating life—if you have one—is spinning out of control, wouldn't you like some basic training so you'll know how to react when things get tough?

Today's dating environment can be relentless, so you have to be prepared. You need to have the right kind of gear, the best field maneuvers, and the determination to succeed. If your goal is not just to date, but to go after the type of relationship that you want and obtain it, you've come to the right place!

So how does this work? Just like a real boot camp, Dating Boot Camp tears you down and builds you back up. First, forget everything you know. The dating rules have changed, so leave what you thought at the door. You will …

♡ Question what others have told you.

♡ Begin to question things yourself.

♡ Strip away the comforts that hold you back, such as always waiting to be noticed or waiting for a guy to act first.

♡ Be pushed to the edge, where you will turn the tables and be the one creating action.

♡ Find strength and confidence you didn't know you had and become the dating powerhouse you didn't know you could be.

Dating Boot Camp gives you the specialized training you need to be successful in the field—without all the combat you've been dealing with. You'll learn how to get "intel" from the other side to gain new insights and a battlefield advantage. You'll learn how not to waste your time on the wrong people by knowing when to engage and when to retreat. Dating Boot Camp gives you the edge you need to be one step ahead of the other troops in the field.

New Rules for a New Dating

The first rule is: Get over yourself! You have to stop blaming yourself for your previous dating failures. If this were 40 years ago, you wouldn't have to create strategies to go after what you want. You would have met your husband through your Aunt Susie or at the neighborhood social gathering. But times have changed. The strong networks once built through our extended family no longer exist. Most people live in isolated communities and rarely interact with their neighbors. Most people have jobs that isolate them even further by demanding more of their time, which pulls them away from their social lives even more. This affects many women, but few do much about it ... except complain.

Even though many women understand that the environment has changed, they still approach dating in the same way. They try to meet men and get dates the way they always have, and get frustrated when it doesn't work. Others feed into the single-woman victim mentality. They say that they don't want to be alone, but rarely want to do the work they need to do to meet more people. Instead, they want sympathy because they are alone and the world is passing them by.

If you want change, then do something to create change. If you keep doing the same thing, you will continuously end up with the same result.

The second rule is: Stop listening to and responding to everything negative around you. Remember, misery loves company, so frustrated people will tell you anything to discourage you. Your job is to filter everything you hear and question its validity. A good soldier knows how to scout for what she needs to know. Here are some common beliefs that can be dispelled:

There Are No Single Men Out There.
Well, if every woman believed that, what would be the point? Single men do exist! However, too many women get discouraged, constantly hearing bleak statements about the dating world that simply aren't true. For instance, how

many of you have heard that the female-to-male dating ratio is 2:1 or even 5:1 in some cases? Well, the alarm is misplaced without the facts.

The U.S. Census Bureau shows that there are 115 unmarried men for every 100 women in their 20s and 30s; it isn't until the 45-to-64 age range that the ratio drops significantly, with only 69 unmarried men for every 100 women.[1] This should help you see that great opportunities are out there—and no matter what your age, the situation isn't as dire as doomsayers might have you believe.

Doing some investigative research will help you know where the best places are to find these guys. *Forbes* magazine does a yearly study on singles in the United States.[2] The following table shows the stats on where they are located.

Top 5 Cities with the Most and Least Number of Singles[2]

Most	Least
Austin, Tex.	Charlotte, N.C.
New Orleans	Kansas City, Mo.
New York	Las Vegas
Los Angeles	Greensboro–Winston Salem, N.C.
San Francisco–Oakland	Tampa, Fla.

There's Nowhere to Go to Meet Single Men.

Some women think that the only place to find eligible men is at a bar. Of course, the bar scene can be, well, dismal at best. However, as *Forbes* reports, the best cities for singles are ranked on a variety of factors, such as nightlife, culture, job growth, and coolness. Don't limit yourself to believing that these singles are only interacting over a beer. The following table shows the best and worst cities to live in if you are single.

Top 5 Best Cities for Singles

Best	Worst
Chicago	Charlotte, N.C.
New York	Greensboro-Winston Salem, N.C.
Miami	Norfolk, Va.
San Diego	Cincinnati
Las Vegas	Pittsburgh

Study based on America's 40 largest metropolitan centers in six different areas: nightlife, culture, job growth, number of other singles, cost of living alone, and coolness.

You Have to Be a Perfect Size 8 to Meet Men.
When you flip on your television, nearly every commercial has a beautiful blonde telling you that you are too fat, too out of shape, too dull, and too unattractive to have a chance at getting the man you want. This is *not* true! Even though you see women running in bikinis and only eating healthy snacks on television, what you see does not represent reality.

The American Society for Testing Materials (ASTM) and Size USA conducted a study to gather data to resize

American clothing.[3] The findings were that the average size for a woman is considered an 8, with ASTM standards listing that size with 37.5-inch hips. Overall, 69 percent of the women in the survey had hips greater than 40 inches, which placed them at a size 12 or 14 rather than a size 8.

What does this prove? That the average woman doesn't look like the women on television. And most men are dating average women. Do the math!

Realize that you have the power to change your experience—your social scene, your dating scene, and your relationships. Your ability to find the right type of relationship for you is about you, not what the media or statistics tell you. Change your perspective and take advantage of every opportunity to get the man that you want.

A Fresh Approach

The dating environment is what it is, so you have to accept that. That does not mean you should cower in the corner and live a dismal existence alone! Instead, study the environment so you'll know how to maneuver through it. A good soldier knows the terrain—to know where the land mines are, where to locate the best supplies, and how to develop a strategy for victory. The dating environment is difficult—so what? People still meet people, your friends still get married, and you still have the opportunity to find a long-lasting relationship with the right man. But you have to change your perspective. The sooner you do that, the sooner you can get what you want.

How do you do this? In essence, you have to start over. Dating Boot Camp will give you a fresh approach to your dating life. You will learn how to date in any environment, no matter how desolate, and find the kind of men you want to date. You will be able to quickly wade through the undesirables so that you don't waste valuable time. Your skills will become so sharp that you will immediately know when a situation isn't working for you and quickly move on.

Not the Easiest Program, but Worth It

This program is not about supporting the victim within. It's about dating empowerment. When you see that you have more control, you realize that you don't need to feel bad about being single. You're not a victim in life, so why become one in dating? You don't have to sit at home waiting for something to change. *Create* change by getting out and doing something to make your life different.

This is not an easy program. It tells you straight-out what you're doing wrong and how you need to fix it. If you want a special relationship, one that grows over the years, you have to be special to another person. How can you be special to someone else when, in a lot of instances, you don't think of yourself as someone special?

As in any boot camp, the Drill Sergeant is your coach. In Dating Boot Camp, she is the voice that pushes you to your limit and makes you get what you need out of the program. The Drill Sergeant wants you to succeed in your dating life. Take her cues, do the drills, and you'll get your badge of honor!

Gaining Control over Your Dating Life

Dating Boot Camp makes you take a hard look at yourself. It makes you question why you aren't happy with yourself, and more importantly, it shows how this unhappiness can sabotage your goals. It's not about changing who you are to get a man interested in you. It's about feeling good about what makes you the person you are and celebrating yourself.

If you read through this book and ignore the exercises and the questions posed to you, then you'll be missing the impact. The woman who successfully gets what she wants is the one who does the work. At times, you're not going to want to do the work. Other times, you're going to push back and ask, "Why do I have to do this?" The truth is, you have to do the work to get the results. This program breaks you down, but when you build yourself back up, you'll be a stronger, more confident you.

The real challenges are those that build your confidence and make you feel empowered. Just think of what it would feel like to go from being the girl who sits around waiting for someone to call on a Saturday night, to being the woman who's out having fun—and when she gets home has two or three desperate messages from men wondering where she is!

You can do it. You can have that control over your dating life. It's time for *you* to choose whom *you* want to date. It's time for *you* to say "no" when you don't want to go out with someone. After all, when you have a few men to choose from, you are the one in control. You pick whom you want—and you may even decide not to pick any of them and go out and meet someone new!

The point is to *enjoy* dating. Dating Boot Camp will make you …

♡ Feel more confident about yourself and more comfortable with who you are.

♡ Learn to take advantage of being single and see it as just another state of being.

♡ Create a single lifestyle that even married people would envy.

♡ Try new things and learn to give yourself permission to do things you've always wanted to do.

♡ Create dating options.

Creating a Road Map for Success

How are you going to accomplish all of this? By actively reading, doing the exercises, and putting time and effort into your project: you. Nobody else can do it for you. However, there are many tools to help you along the way:

♡ **Challenges and objectives.** Each chapter gives you a clear idea of what you need to accomplish and what main challenge you need to master.

♡ **Personal assessment exercises.** These exercises give you an opportunity to check in with yourself, to see what you need to know more about and provide you with more learning about yourself.

♡ **Creating an action plan.** Here you get the opportunity to build a tactical plan to help guide you from where you are now to your ultimate goal of a full dating life. These steps get you closer to the long-term relationship you desire.

♡ **Action activities.** In addition to the action plan, you need to complete additional activities. The tasks are given in an easy-to-follow fashion with do's and don'ts to review.

♡ **Role of the Drill Sergeant.** The Drill Sergeant is with you every step of the way. As you read, you might notice that the tone of the Drill Sergeant is pretty direct. The Drill Sergeant is your coach and gives you guidance. Remember, the Drill Sergeant's main objective is not to be nice, but to get you through boot camp!

♡ **Drill Sergeant Says.** In addition to the commentary and directions from the Drill Sergeant, you will also find points or tips that the Drill Sergeant wants to highlight in various areas. Again, even if they seem harsh, they're meant to help you get through your training.

Now that you have enlisted, it's time to report to Dating Boot Camp!

Endnotes

[1] As reported by Lisa Takeuchi Cullen, "Cupid Academy," *Time*, February 16, 2004.

[2] *Forbes*, June 25, 2004.

[3] *The Christian Science Monitor*, March 4, 2004.

2

Where You Are Today and What's Not Working

As a new boot camp recruit, before you begin any kind of training, you do an assessment to understand where you are now. How else would you measure your progress at the end? An assessment of where you are today will give you insight into why you don't have the kind of relationship success you want, and help you determine if something is holding you back. You might not think you could be hindering your own success, but *you* are a bigger factor in this equation than you think.

Here is where boot camp begins. You need to be broken down to find out what might be holding you back. Do you have a severe lack of confidence? Do you believe that men don't find you attractive, or that you're just not their type? Are you holding on to some old relationship baggage that's preventing you from getting close to anyone?

Before U.S. Marine recruits pass boot camp, they must successfully complete an obstacle course that includes a rope climb over a wall. Many recruits get intimidated just looking at it, but they know they have to make it over the wall in order to complete their training. It's hard and grueling and will take everything out of them, but they push themselves to the limit to make it over. When they do, they have a sense of completion and a feeling that they can deal with any other obstacle that comes their way. Right now, you are facing your rope climb. Don't let it intimidate you. Just picture yourself standing on the other side.

Taking the time to uncover your blocks will ultimately make you more successful in your next relationship. Even though it may be painful, you'll be glad you learned what is keeping you from happiness. Once you do this, you can start moving forward. You'll be proud you pushed through this drill—and you'll be better for it in the end!

Why Aren't You Getting What You Want?

If you survey most women, they'll tell you that all the good men are either married, poor, gay, or have too many children. The perception that there's a shortage of males is common among single women, but there's a flip side.

Most women don't believe it when a desirable man says it's hard for him to meet a good woman, but unfortunately, it's true. There are good men out there who can't meet the good women they want to be with. These men want to be married, with a family, a home, and someone to come home to every night. So why aren't you meeting these men if you're both looking for the same things? What is the problem?

Believe it or not, some men find the dating scene just as frustrating as you do and are having trouble finding Ms. Right for themselves. They want women who understand them, but feel that they are few and far between. Here are some perspectives from a survey of the other side's encampment[1]:

♡ Men aren't great verbal communicators. They don't relate to women who aren't direct and to the point.

♡ Men don't like women who pretend to be something they're not. Being sexy and encouraging is good, but when it's not genuine, it's a turnoff.

♡ Men don't like it when women share their feelings too early.

However, men do communicate their feelings nonverbally in four areas:

♡ Socially: Where the man is at in his own life—stability, confidence, and direction

♡ Emotionally: Whether or not he's "emotionally available"

♡ Physically: If he's attractive and attracted to a woman

♡ In the love state: If he's open to building and growing a relationship

When women misread these important signals, a man is turned off. What turns men off the most?

♡ When women expect to be taken care of

♡ When women try to convince men to like or love them

♡ When women try to win a man's heart through sex

Honey, Will You Get the Bags?
As easy as it might be to blame everything on the guys, women have to take equal responsibility when relationships don't work out. It's not easy to see, but baggage from past relationships can be damaging your chances at future ones.

At first, the end of a relationship can be painful to think about. If you don't address it, and the reasons for it, this pain can bury itself deep inside your heart. You won't even know it's there until a similar situation arises, or you start to fear getting hurt again. You aren't even aware this baggage is weighing you down until your guy says the wrong thing and you dump it all out on his head.

In boot camp, those of you with the heaviest baggage are the ones who'll want to drop out. You'll blame the program, saying it's too hard, when in fact the pain is too deep or too grueling to face. Commit to dealing with your baggage so you can finally leave it at home. Once you make the commitment, you won't believe how much lighter your pack will be.

Why does this so often hold women back? Women may have more relationship baggage than men because they have more relationships. On top of that, their baggage is loaded with extra negative messages from their mothers, other women, and even the media—all telling them that they're a failure if they aren't successful in love.

You may also unknowingly stuff more junk in your baggage when you buy into negative images that make you feel bad about yourself. You end up carrying around all this extra weight. Worse, it may be interfering with a relationship you're in currently. You may find it's not that you don't want a relationship, but you might be subconsciously preventing yourself from getting one.

At boot camp, you get assigned a pack full of gear to hike around with. Is it heavy? Yes. But is everything in there necessary? Yes. Do you want to keep unnecessary, unauthorized stuff in your pack or your footlocker? No! Dating Boot Camp helps you strip down to the essentials. You carry just what you need, even if it's heavy, and let go of anything unnecessary—like past hurts, slights, and anger.

Make It Happen!

What's weighing down your duffel bag? Lighten it up by examining the stuff left from your last five relationships. Look at it, deal with it, and *let it go!* Here are some questions to help you do this:

- Even if you have no contact with your ex, do you constantly talk about how he hurt you?

continues

continued

- Are you mad at someone that you dated, but can't talk it out with him?
- Do you feel that men will always treat you badly?
- Did your ex move on to another relationship, but you can't seem to?
- Do you feel that someone took advantage of or used you?
- Were you mentally or physically abused by someone?

If you answered "Yes" to any of these questions, these are the things that you need to purge. Go back over the situation. Is there a way to resolve it with the person or within yourself? Talk or write a letter to the person involved. Write down some thoughts about the situation for yourself. Do whatever you need to do to work through it so you can stop hurting and move on.

Now, what's in your duffel that you're really going to need?

- Good communication skills
- Openness
- Ability to share
- Honesty
- Forgiveness
- Love

You'll have more room for these things if you get rid of all that unnecessary junk!

Ending the Self-Sabotage

Kim had a series of relationships that ended in the same place: nowhere. Kim had a great job as a photographer

*and just bought a loft for her living and workspace.
She had a lot to offer, and couldn't understand why her
relationships never lasted more than a couple months.
She asked her close friend Todd for his opinion. Kim
learned that she had a habit of expecting relationship-
type commitment from her dates way too early. She
hadn't realized it, but Todd was right. She wanted a
relationship so badly that she didn't even see it. Kim
knew she had to deal with this or she would never
have the kind of relationship that she wanted.*

It is a hard realization to know that you could have had a
big hand in the demise of your own relationships. Even
though the truth may be hard to stomach, you have to face
it. To stop the self-sabotage, you need to think through
your contributing factors. The point is not to fix blame,
but to address the situation so you can learn to deal with
similar circumstances differently in the future. Take some
time to think about the following:

♡ When you disagree with a significant other, do you
   scream or yell at him?

♡ When you don't like something he's done, do you nag
   about it constantly? Or do you give him the silent
   treatment?

♡ Do you find it hard to forgive people?

21

♡ Do you try to control a situation if it's not going your way?

♡ Do you need to have your way most of the time? Do you believe in compromise?

♡ Do you feel that, most of the time, your significant other is wrong?

Be honest with yourself and answer the questions truthfully! Then get some input on the topic from the people who know you best. Ask a trusted girlfriend, a close male friend, an ex-boyfriend, dating adviser, or counselor. Don't shy away from this, because it can either justify your answers or help you see something about yourself that you were completely unaware of.

Make It Happen!

Take this quiz to find out if you are self-sabotaging your own relationships.

1. Does every relationship you have end up in the same argument? (Such as, he doesn't spend enough time with you, or he doesn't seem as interested in you as you are in him.)

2. Have the last few men you dated said they have a hard time dealing with the same thing? (Such as, you are too controlling, you talk about yourself too much, or you wanted more than they could give so early in the relationship.)

3. Do you tend to always pick the same type of man to date?

4. Would most of your friends say that the men you choose are the wrong type of person for you?

5. Would *you* say the men you choose are the wrong type of men for you?

6. Do you feel that there is anything you could do to help make your relationships work better?

7. Do you feel resentful about your past relationships not working out?

8. Do you think men are fundamentally incapable of having a relationship?

9. Do you think all men are just dogs?

10. Do you think all men will eventually lie or cheat on you?

11. Do you think that you really can't have a great relationship and you are lucky to have anyone you get?

12. If you were in a relationship, would your life be much happier?

13. Do you think you have to be attractive to have a relationship?

14. If you looked better, do you think you would have a happier relationship?

If you answered "Yes" to more than two of these questions, then you definitely need to do a little soul-searching.

Are You Picking the Wrong Types of Guys?

If you're honest about what's lurking deep down inside you, you may find a few common problems that are sabotaging your relationships. If you always try to change the men you date, that's a problem. If you expect your relationships to always be perfect, that's a problem. If your relationships keep failing in the same way and you never see that you share some of the blame, that's a problem.

At some point, you have to identify for yourself what's going wrong. Maybe it is the men you choose. If you keep making bad picks for yourself, then you are doomed to fail before you even start. Bad picks are something that *you* control; acknowledging your role helps keep you from starting your next relationship with the wrong person.

It's possible that you can't break a pattern simply because it's what you're used to. That doesn't say anything bad about you, but it shows that you need to shake things up.

Make It Happen!

Think about your last five relationships. Take the quiz below to help you determine if you are meeting Mr. Wrong:

1. Do you typically date a certain type of guy?

2. Is this type compatible with your relationship goals?

3. Did the men you were involved with pursue the relationship, or did you?

---

4. Did you tend to hope for the best but expected the worst in your relationships?

5. Were these guys financially stable? Could they take care of themselves?

6. Were they emotionally stable or emotionally draining?

7. Do you only date attractive men? If "Yes," do you like the attention you get when you do?

8. Have you had a good relationship with someone who didn't match your usual type?

9. Ask three girlfriends what your type is. Do they all say the same thing?

10. Do you feel that you date certain types of men for a reason?

After you answer all of the questions, ask yourself what the similarities are between your ex-boyfriends. If these relationships ended poorly, are there similarities? If the answer is "Yes," you may need to reassess whom you are dating.

Acknowledge Your Demons

Jasmine was always afraid that she would end up alone. Every time she was in a relationship with a cool guy, she would eventually start fearing that he was going to leave her. When she felt this way, she would start calling him all the time. If he said he was going to the store, she would call to make sure he was not lying. If he didn't call her exactly when he

said he would, she would panic and keep calling him until she reached him. Every time, Jasmine's fear became a reality: The men would leave her and she would be alone again. Jasmine knew that this was a problem but continued to not deal with it.

Everyone has something about themselves they do not feel great about. However, when you're in a relationship (or want to be), your demon can rear its ugly head and cause problems. Be strong and deal with what might be keeping you from getting the relationship you want. Dealing with it now will help you to move on and feel good about yourself.

If you know that your demon will more than likely surface, why keep hiding it, waiting for it to come out? It may seem easier to avoid addressing it in the short run, but you'll have more to lose in the long run. Stop hiding under the bunker and address it once and for all. Remember, focusing on your personal issues is about you, first and foremost. The sooner you go through the process, the sooner you can feel good about you. The better you feel about you, the closer you will get to meeting the right person!

Make It Happen!

If you're serious about not letting your demons ambush your relationships, take some time to work through the problem. Following are resources that may help:

- **Private counseling.** Many people have a lot of child-hood secrets they've never addressed which become bigger problems in adulthood. Find someone you feel comfortable with to talk to about these issues.

- **Support groups.** There are groups to help you get assistance for even the most challenging issues. Groups range from people wanting to find daily happiness to people dealing with alcoholic loved ones. Find one that works for you.

- **Spiritual counseling.** Some people feel more comfortable speaking to someone in their church, such as a reverend, priest, or clergyman.

- **Self-help.** There are self-help books on every topic you can think of. Go to the bookstore or search online. Most of these books help you with therapy through writing and shared experience.

New and Improved

Candice always felt self-conscious when she went out with her girlfriends to meet men. She was a little chunky around the middle and it made her clothes fit funny. She wasn't really overweight, she just had a love-handle problem. Candice knew she could go to the gym and probably work it off, but never really made the effort. Still, she always felt bad about herself when other men would approach her friends to

*dance or to chat and not her. She knew that it was
probably her attitude more than her love-handle issue
that made the men stay away, but it sure felt more
like her love handles.*

When you've begun figuring out what you need to work
on, you'll be moving toward a more successful relationship.
While you're at it, is there something about yourself that you
would like to improve? Is there a characteristic you'd like to
bring out more—or something you'd like to see less of?

It's up to you to drive your self-improvement goals. No
one is advocating that you change who you are to meet men.
Instead, look at it from this standpoint: You are enhancing
yourself to be the best you can be, which will show in all
of your future interactions with men. You cannot change
yourself for anyone and shouldn't.

However, when you don't deal with a problem, it doesn't
go away. The longer you wait to deal with it, the longer
you're denying yourself what you want. Create a plan to
address and resolve your issues. You are the only person
who knows what you need and the only one who can put
the plan into action! More than likely, your problem isn't
as big as you're making it out to be, and the boost your
self-esteem will get from addressing it will be greater than
the problem ever was.

Remember that you control what you do. Why be a victim and feel bad about something you can change? If you
don't feel good about the way your love handles look, then

do something about them! Get to the gym and work on that problem area. Get some fashion advice, identify the best look for your body type, and enhance your look. If you wake up feeling unattractive, wear a flattering, colorful outfit and buy yourself some flowers on the way to work.

Many times, what you think people perceive about you is inaccurate. You may think you look fat, but other people probably don't think so. However, you're telling them you are through your demeanor. *You* control your feelings, your problems, and your outlook. Use the resources around you to solve your issues. Even if it's something you can't change overnight, taking steps in that direction will make you feel great. Do whatever it takes to feel better and more confident about yourself. The more you do, the more people will notice.

Know What You Want

> *Nancy decided that she didn't want to be the token single guest any longer. She went out and met Ralph. She wasn't really head-over-heels for him, but at least he was nice and she could bring him around her friends. Nancy dated Ralph for about six months and eventually got bored with him, but she didn't want to break up. She just couldn't stand the frustration of being alone again. However, Ralph was really start-ing to get on her nerves ....*

Most single women say they want to be in a relationship. As a result, many are afraid to rule anyone out, so they end up spending too much time dragging along in dead-end relationships. They date guys who were all wrong to begin with when they should have just said, "This is not what I want."

In order to get what you need, it's important to know what you really want. Do you want someone a little different, to be a good balance for you? Or do you need someone just like you so that the two of you get along well? Thinking about this now will save you both time and heartaches in the end.

A lot of people stay with someone for the sake of not being alone, but just getting a warm body to hang out with you only solves part of the problem. If you're not happy with that person, you're still going to yearn for something more. There's a certain comfort in being in a relationship with someone, but wouldn't it be much more amazing to find the *right* person to be with?

It's better to be single, enjoy yourself, and have the freedom to find the right person for you. Doesn't that sound better than waking up to someone you don't like every day? Think about what you're really looking for in a man so you can choose one who's a good fit for you.

Get a Clear Picture of the Man You Want

If you were looking for a particular outfit to wear to a function, you could probably envision what you want to look like. Even if you can't exactly picture the dress, you have a good idea of how it should fit, how it should make you look, and how stunning the right outfit can make you feel.

Finding the right man is similar. You might not be able to picture exactly what he looks like, but you should have a vague idea of how you want him to look, in addition to the qualities you want him to possess. You're probably not going to find someone with *all* of the characteristics you're looking for, but the right man for you should at least possess the characteristics that are most important.

Write down what these qualities are and rank them in order of importance. Taking the time to make this list might help you discover that you'd actually prefer a guy who's less than successful but is kind and sweet over a real go-getter who's edgy and pompous. Do the work so that you know what you're truly looking for.

Make It Happen!

Build the profile of what you are looking for in a man by ranking which qualities are most important to you. Use this list as you meet eligible men.

continues

continued

Characteristics Most Important to You

(Rank each on a scale of 1–5, with 1 being most important.)

Characteristic	Rank of Importance
Provides for his family	
Fun	
Adventurous	
Smart	
Generous	
Driven	
Romantic	
Gregarious	
Caring	
Educated	
Athletic	
Laid-back	
Well-traveled	
Conscientious	
Attractive	
Well-read	
Handsome	
Artistic	
Professional	
Rugged	
Tenacious	
Stable	

Characteristic	Rank of Importance
Wealthy	
Racy	
Settled	
Patient	
Sincere	
Good father	
Bad boy	
Religious	
Mannerly	
Reliable	
Trustworthy	
Determined	
Shy	
Responsible	
Fashionable	
Clever	
Experienced	
Earthy	
Concerned	
Doughty	
Sweet	
Spiritual	
Nature-oriented	
Life of the party	

continues

continued

Characteristics Most Important to You

Characteristic	Rank of Importance
Attention-getting	
Creative	
Stoic	
Loving	

Narrow your list by grouping your 1s and 2s on another page. Read through this new list and rerank anything that you see fit. Rank the 1s from most important to least important. Narrow this list even further by circling the five most important items. Do a temperature check. Is this how you have been selecting your men? If not, realize that what you have identified as the top five most important characteristics should be what you are seeking. Take this list with you the next time you're out meeting people. Use this criteria and notice the difference in the kind of men you meet!

Endnote

[1] *Catch Him ... and Keep Him*, eReport, Mark Matthews, August 2004.

3

Starting Your New Regimen

Now that you've enlisted and taken a look at where you are in your dating life, it's time to develop a plan for moving toward where you would like to be. This may sound like extra work, and it is ... but it's well worth it. No one said this was going to be easy; boot camp never is. However, once you put in the time, you'll see the benefit of your efforts. Develop your action plan, and your goals—and the best way to reach them—will be clear.

In this process, you will tear down your old self and build a stronger and better you. The more you are involved, the better it will be. So get ready to do the training drills!

Part 1—Create Your Action Plan

Think of your action plan as a road map. You have a destination and you need to know the best way to get there. Mapping out where you want to go will help you stay on course with the dating milestones you wish to achieve. Put serious thought into your action plan, because it is the framework for your training.

Your action plan has three parts. The first part will help you identify things about yourself that you may want to change or improve. The second part will help you put efforts in place to make these changes. Parts 2 and 3 are covered later in the book. It won't be an easy process, but if you do it well, it can be the most rewarding exercise. Commit to doing the work and work at these training drills. If you follow through, the rewards will be amazing.

Identify Your Stumbling Blocks

Identifying what you would like to be different in your life is the first and most important step in your assessment. The difficulty of getting inside yourself can break down even the strongest person. You have to face your fears in order to deal with them. Once you acknowledge what you need to do and then do it, you will be able to do anything! More importantly, by dealing with the things that hold you back, you will be ready to take on any dating challenge. Your confidence will be stronger and men will definitely notice.

In Chapter 2, you began to think about what holds you back from achieving what you want in your dating life. Note which areas you want to focus on to improve your dating outlook. Following are areas of consideration:

Your appearance. What are you unhappy with?

♡ Your weight

♡ Your body

♡ Your hair

♡ Your style

♡ Your shyness around others

♡ Your confidence level

♡ Your overall presentation

Your attitude ...

♡ Is negative in general

♡ Shows that you are not content with your life

♡ Needs a severe readjustment

♡ Reflects badly on you when you meet men

♡ Protects you from being hurt

Your desire to make your dating life better ...

♡ Is generally low

♡ Can vary depending on the sense of urgency

♡ Changes only when completely necessary

Address What You Would Like to Change/Enhance
Decide what you want to work on to break out of the stagnation you are experiencing. Complete the sentences below:

1. I would like to change the following about myself:

_____

_____

2. If I were able to change _____, I would feel better about myself.

3. If _____ were different, I would feel more comfortable meeting other people.

Look at the list. This is the framework for your program. You have identified the problems and addressed what you would like to change. The next step is to create a strategy that will help you get past your blockage, listing ways to help you get there and following through on these actions. After you go through this process, you will have finished the work.

Make It Happen!

In order to get to the next level, you need to be specific about how you are going to get there. Here are some steps on how to do this:

1. On a piece of paper, write down your personal goal.

2. Under the personal goal, write down what you are going to gain when you achieve this goal.

3. Brainstorm and write down the hurdles that you see in achieving this goal.

4. Narrow this list down to three hurdles that you want to focus on.

5. Find actionable solutions. For instance, list an activity that you can do, a seminar or class that you can attend, or other actions that you can actively participate in to address the hurdle.

6. Once you have done this, put your work to the test by getting out in the field and seeing how differently you respond to your previous problem.

Setting goals helps you get through any challenge you face. The key is to break down your issue so you can see the steps you need to take to get to success. If you want to lose weight, identify how much you would like to lose, find a diet program that works for you, and follow your diet. If you want to dress better, identify the look you want to achieve, hit the right stores, get a personal shopper, and learn what clothing and accessory combinations work for you. Whatever your goal, you can do the work to get out of the trenches and combat anything that is in your way to success!

Decide What You Want and Go for It

Many women find that, after a while, dating can make you feel like you're in the middle of a battlefield. Going through repeated trial and error, it seems to be more trouble than it's worth. Part of the problem is that some women aren't sure what kind of relationship they want, so they end up in relationships with people who don't want what they want. As a result, a lot of women feel that what they are looking for is not out there.

You have to believe that the relationship that you want is obtainable. Just because this magical union hasn't developed by now doesn't mean it *can't*. There are too many instances of women finding love when they least expected it. Talented and beautiful *Pretty Woman* star Julia Roberts had a number of failed relationships. Now she is happily married to a wonderful man and is having twins! One minute there wasn't a man for *The View*'s Star Jones, then suddenly she's in love. Breaking all the stereotypes that fairy tales only happen if you are perfect size 6, Star Jones got engaged to her beau at the NBA All-Star game on national television.

These women wanted special relationships, and that's what, in the end, they got. Fame, beauty, or fortune didn't matter for them, and it shouldn't for you. Belief and confidence in getting what you want is more important. The key is to be direct about the type of relationship you want and the kind of person you're willing to get involved with. Focus your energy in the right place and the relationship you want will formulate.

Ann knew that she wanted to find a special person to make a commitment to. She wanted to eventually get married and have a child. Ann went to a singles mixer and met Leon. She and Leon had a number of things in common and Ann thought it was a good match. However, Leon didn't want children because he already had two of his own. Ann was sure that Leon would eventually be open to having a child with her if they

got married. A few years went by and Leon proposed, but he made it clear to Ann that he still didn't want to have any more children. Ann couldn't compromise on what she wanted and eventually left the relationship.

Don't be railroaded into giving up something important just to be with someone. There is a difference between compromise and accepting something you don't want. Be clear on what you need and expect from your relationship. Your partner should respect your wishes, and if it's something that you cannot compromise on, you may need to rethink your relationship. Too often women will just accept something that they don't want to make their partner happy. The right person wouldn't ask you to do this. State your needs, and if the person you're dating doesn't hear you out, know that someone else will.

Define What a Relationship Means to You
If you could have the ideal relationship, what would it look like? Is it a scene right out of *Love Story*, or more like *When Harry Met Sally*? Would your ideal relationship be fun and playful most of the time? Or would it be deeply loving and intense? Whatever you envision, it is up to you to define what you want and then go after it.

Evaluate your past relationships. What were the elements that meant the most to you? Did you mostly enjoy quiet times with your partner? Or did you like getting out and about together and having fun? Make a compilation in your mind of these moments and make them part of your relationship wish list. You may not get everything you like, but at least you will know what you want going in.

Make It Happen!

If you had the opportunity to build the perfect relationship, what would it entail? Note what elements of a relationship are important to you and incorporate them into your next relationship search:

- You have a forum to talk about your problems
- You have someone with whom to share your secrets
- Your partner is supportive of all of your endeavors
- If you have an argument, you can talk through it
- You can be honest about your true feelings
- Your partner sees you for who you truly are
- You both want the same things
- You share couple time, but also make time for your own interests
- You give each other the space that you need any time that you need it
- You have a spiritual connection with one another
- You share quality time and understand the value of it in your relationship
- You are physically attracted to one another
- You have passionate lovemaking sessions

- You can share any emotion necessary in front of your partner and not feel bad about it
- You both can learn and grow together
- You enjoy the same things
- You are best friends

In the previous chapter, you selected desired qualities in a person you would like to date. In this chapter, you selected qualities in a relationship that you want to have. In both cases, it is up to you to determine the deal-breakers and priorities. Maybe you are with a guy who treats you like a princess most of the time, but has been unfaithful in your relationship. Or maybe your guy is a great lover but never wants to hang out with your friends. You have to decide what mix of qualities works best for you in a long-term romance. Remember, this is your journey, and you are in control of things you do and don't want to accept.

Determining Your Dating Readiness

When you think about dating, what comes to mind? Do you immediately groan, thinking about how painful it can be? Or do you look forward to meeting people and having fun? Your attitude will determine how ready you are to step into the dating arena and how you will proceed on your dating journey. Having a positive outlook on the adventure you're about to have can help bring more positive experiences your way. Whether it has been a long time or you're just getting a fresh start, get ready for your new dating experience!

Make It Happen!

Only you can determine how ready you are to get out there. Gear yourself up by thinking about the reasons why you would like to date. You want to ...

- Meet new people.
- Have fun things to do.
- Make new friends.
- Meet someone special.
- Have a long-term relationship.
- Get married.
- Have a family with someone.
- Break the monotony.
- Feel good about being single.
- Feel less alone.
- Enjoy your life.

Putting Your Plan into Action

You have now laid the groundwork for the next phase of boot camp. Now it's time to put your plan into effect. The next phase of your training involves working on *you*. Some areas will be easier to deal with than others, and you might get frustrated and think this is all too hard.

Keep thinking about the rewards you will receive and you will stay motivated. By taking on this personal project, you will feel better about yourself and potentially end up with someone you really want to be with. It's time to let go of those old habits and head for the goal you want.

Part 2

BOOT CAMP
Basic Training

4

Putting Your Plan into Action

Now that you have completed a personal assessment, you should have a better feeling about what might be keeping you from having a successful relationship. You also have targeted some factors you'd like to see in a partner and in a relationship. And on the radar, you've even set goals and come up with an action plan.

Now it's time to put that plan into action. It won't be easy to change things that you have been dealing with for perhaps your whole dating life. This is where you're going to feel the burn, but don't worry, soldier, you can do it! Your new regimen will be challenging, but you will come out of the trenches an improved woman. You came to Dating Boot Camp to get results, and here is where you're going to make it happen!

Sometimes Looks *Do* Matter

These training drills to enhance yourself are not about changing who you are to get a man. They are about doing whatever you need to do to feel better about yourself so you can get the man you want.

It's just a fact that men are more visual than women are, and beauty on the outside usually attracts them before they see your beauty on the inside. You can be the coolest chick in the world, but if you aren't doing anything to get noticed, you may get overlooked. Right or wrong, that's the way it is. This doesn't mean you have to entirely change what you look like to get noticed, but it does mean you should enhance what you have. Get out of the camouflage and make him notice you. Once he does, your great attributes can do the rest.

In many cases, you aren't really changing yourself—you are just polishing up the package. Everyone knows that shiny packages get noticed. Even so, some women are made to feel guilty by family, friends, peers, and even society if they decide to focus on their looks. They're told that they are being shallow. If you have always wanted to change your nose, or if you think just fixing it would make you more confident and happy, then get your nose done! There is no reason not to feel good about how you look. You're not shallow; you just want to feel better about yourself.

It's time to stop talking about what you wish you looked like and take the steps to look the way you want. You've spent too much time not being noticed or feeling bad about not getting what you want. Stop hiding behind the excuses and deal with it. Lay out your plan, do the work, and get to your goal. The following sections help you shed those extra pounds, change your look, and shake up your attitude.

Drill Sergeant Says ...

Only you can decide what is going to make you feel better to help you stand out in the crowd. Whether you want to enhance your body or add color into your wardrobe, making these changes will help you to feel more confident and it will show. Make others around you take notice!

Feel Good at Any Weight

Mikki was a very attractive girl, but she was constantly told that she was just too heavy for her height. All of her life she was teased about her weight—which made her gain more weight. Men rarely approached Mikki, and when they did, she immediately thought they would not want to go out with her. Mikki ate through her frustration and continued to gain weight. Eventually, Mikki stopped going out with her friends and didn't care about dating, meeting men, or much of anything else.

Extra weight is one of the biggest excuses women make for why they're dissatisfied with their dating life. It's easy to hide behind weight and say, "I'll never get a date," which later becomes "I will never get a date and I don't care."

Listen to me, girls: This is the ultimate cop-out. It's actually *easier* to not lose weight and not deal with your unhappiness. It's easier to not try, to wear big clothes, and not make an effort to look good. Yes, diets are hard. Passing up food that you like is hard. Shopping for clothes you look good in at any weight is hard. But in the long run, won't wishing you looked a certain way and never getting there be even harder?

There's no magic formula to feeling good about your weight. There's also no magic diet or exercise program; otherwise, everyone would be thin. You have to decide how you feel about your weight, and don't let other people make you feel bad for your choices. The people who lose weight are the ones who put the time and energy into dieting and exercise. Those who don't either accept who they are and feel happier for it, or they blame everything else for their weight problem.

These are your options, and only you can decide what is best for you. If your decision is to lose those pounds—either a few or a lot—know that it will be hard work. The effort you put into saying it is hard is the same effort you should put into being successful at it. There is no quick fix.

It takes time, effort, and constant motivation to get those extra pounds off.

Losing a few pounds may help you feel better about the 20 or 50 you didn't lose. The key is for you to feel good about yourself. If you think you look beautiful, other people will, too. And if you won't feel beautiful until you can fit in that little black dress, then go for it!

Only you can determine what size makes you feel good. You can look good at whatever size you are. Don't hide behind big clothes; find clothes that enhance your body type. There are fashionable options for women at any size. Toss clothes that make you feel dowdy. Go out and buy a sassy new skirt or sleeveless top. Play up all of your physical attributes. If you have nice legs, flaunt them. If you have an enviable chest, enhance it. Buy clothes that show off your best parts and help you feel sexy. It's not always about being the skinniest girl—some men will say outright that they don't like skinny women! What's most important is for you to do what you need to do to get to a size that makes you look and feel good—whatever size that is.

Make It Happen!

If you have decided to lose weight, then get ready for battle. Not every program is going to work for everybody, so create a program that works best for you.

continues

continued

Don't ...

- Get frustrated about how much you have to lose. Break your big goal into little chunks so it feels more manage- able.
- Create setbacks for yourself by going off your diet.
- Worry about how others are doing—keep the focus on you.

Do ...

- Identify how much weight you want to lose.
- Ask a doctor to help find the best program for you.
- Determine your method to get the weight off. Whether you do it on your own or follow a program such as Weight Watchers, Atkins, or the South Beach Diet, pick one and get started.
- Set a goal for how long it will take to lose the extra 5, 10, 20 pounds or more.
- Keep a log of what you are doing every day to reach your goal. Be sure to write down what physical activity you do.
- Cross off each day on your calendar as you work at it until you reach your goal.

- Celebrate when you get to any milestone that you have set. Reward yourself for every 5 pounds you lose as you get closer to your goal; for example, buy a new shirt or lipstick, or plan a fun evening out.

Losing weight is one of the hardest things to do. Keep in mind that the longer you put off feeling good, the less time you'll have to get the man you want. Some of you will say that the right man will love you regardless. He *will*, but not if you don't give him the chance to meet you. If you're obsessing about not losing weight, he may pass you by. Lose the weight, lose the guilt, and quit hiding yourself.

Be a Gym Chick
You used to work out all the time and it felt so good, but now you're just too busy with work. And while a diet would be okay, you really just need to tone up. It doesn't matter what your age is, you can always look your best in anything that you wear. The key is to be fit. If you want to feel your best, it's time to visit your local aerobics class.

Exercise is about a lot more than losing weight. Certainly, it's a strong component to a weight loss program, but exercise for its own sake can make you feel better, have more energy, and keep your stress levels down.

There are many ways to get fit. You can join a gym that has aerobic, strengthening, or toning classes. Bike riding, yoga, and Pilates are all ways you can change up your workout routine without getting bored. If you're really serious, you can hire a trainer to help you with your trouble spots. Just get off the couch and move. Whatever you choose, just do something.

Beginning a new exercise program is not just about getting a date. Exercising will make you look better, feel better, and have more stamina for your busy new social life. As an added plus, you may even meet someone at the gym that you want to go out with! The benefits outweigh the excuses, so put a plan in place and make it happen.

Make It Happen!

Whether you want to enhance your weight-loss efforts or just get up and move, creating an active lifestyle will make you feel good.

Don't...

- Overdo it. Don't expect to be Miss Aerobic Fitness in a day. Start slow and add more to your program over time.

- Just follow a routine. Get a trainer to design a regimen that is best for your capabilities and body type.

- Compete—this is about you and your goals, no one else's. Remember, you are trying to be the best you can be, not better than everybody else in the gym.

- Get discouraged. Turn this thinking around by focusing on your improvements. The more you keep at it, the more you will get results.

Do ...

- Determine what your exercise goal is—toning up in general, fitting into your swimsuit, or looking like you work out.
- Identify how and where you want your activity to take place: at a gym, at home, outside, with another person, in a group, or solo.
- Guesstimate how long it will take you to reach your goal, then track it.
- Get someone to take before and after pictures of you so you can see your own progress.
- Figure out what exercise is fun so you will enjoy it and stick with it.
- Get a workout buddy to help you stay motivated.
- Remember all of the benefits of your workout plan.

What if you're interested in exercising, but you aren't really the "gym type"? You don't have to be. Exercising is simply about moving your body, and you can do it anywhere! Make exercising fun by getting some of your friends together for some outdoor sports. Take a dance class at a studio in your area. You can even shake it up at home by cleaning up or just moving vigorously around the house. Here are some ideas to keep your program going:

♡ Walking. Taking a walk is the easiest way to get started on an exercise program. Start in your neighborhood and then move to an area with walking trails or a track.

♡ Bike riding. Grab your bicycle out of the garage and take it for a spin. Bike riding is an activity that you can do with friends or your children.

♡ Hiking. Experience nature and get some good exercise in, too, by going on a hike. Trails vary in length and difficulty, so explore the different hiking opportunities in your area.

♡ Yoga. There are many forms of yoga, and the best place to find a variety is at a yoga studio. Yoga is a great form of exercising and you are guaranteed to shape up and de-stress.

♡ Dance classes. Exercising doesn't always have to be about strict movement and routines. Take a salsa, ballroom, African, or modern dance class to have fun and tone up.

♡ Housework. Cut your exercise time in half by cleaning to some upbeat dance tunes to get you sweating.

♡ Exercise tapes. You can make your home into an exercise haven by working out to various exercise videos.

You can take fun classes like kickboxing, dance, aerobics, or resistance training, all in your own living room.

♡ Exercise clubs. Look online to find different exercise groups in your neighborhood. Some folks are looking for an exercise buddy, while others need new members for the morning Tai Chi sessions.

Try a New Look

Desiree was always self-conscious about her saddlebags. She worked out and dieted, but nothing made them go away. Finally, a friend suggested plastic surgery. Desiree had always believed that people should be happy the way God made them ... but she wasn't happy. So she decided to have the surgery and soon felt that her life changed. She felt better about her body and decided to buy a new wardrobe. The new wardrobe led into her getting a makeover and new haircut. Desiree felt so good about herself that it was no wonder she had more dates than she could juggle. Getting rid of her saddlebags helped Desiree love herself again!

We all read fashion magazines, whether it's *Vogue, Cosmo*, or *Glamour*, and we all have looked at those women and said, "I'll bet she doesn't have any trouble getting dates."

Well, she might, you never know. Even models have trouble dating sometimes. But the look and style is what the media train men to want, and women to want to have. Does that mean you have to bow to their ideas and spend money you don't have on hair, clothes, and makeup? No, of course not. However, it does mean that you have to accept, to some degree, that in order to play in this often competitive dating market, you have to look your best. And besides, a whole new look is not a bad thing to have.

In the age of the makeover, you can change anything about yourself to look perfect. No one is advocating perfection; however, a minor overhaul couldn't hurt. You don't have to be the latest runway fashion plate, but you can do things that help you to stand out a little bit more in a crowd. Get a trendy haircut, wear the new makeup color, and upgrade your wardrobe with a new handbag or shoes.

Make It Happen!

Freshening up your look is one of the easiest ways to change your appearance and your attitude. Simple adjustments can have a major impact. To get started, follow these steps:

1. Make a list of the things that you could do to feel more fashionable. Break this list into three categories: makeup, hair, and clothes.

2. In each section, write down what you would like to see for yourself in each area.

3. Put a date by each of these sections and make a goal to accomplish one of these each week.

Don't ...

- Try to turn yourself into the cover of *Cosmo*.

- Feel as though you have to spend a lot of money to get the results that you want.

- Make extreme changes if you're not ready to change.

Do ...

- Get references. If you like something about your friends, ask them for their hair stylist's phone number or where they purchased a particular outfit.

- Get resources. There are many beauty and fashion experts who offer advice in the top women's magazines and online.

- Try your local department store for fashion help. Some stores offer the services of a personal shopper. This person can help find flattering outfits for you and a lot of times their services are free.

- Sign up for a free makeover at a department store or beauty outlet. Ask the makeup technician to give you tips for both day and evening looks.

- Change your hair! Before you walk into a salon, find a look that you want and bring a picture with you. Ask the

continues

continued

stylist if the look will enhance your face and, if not, what she would suggest. You may find that you don't need a cut, but a spruce-up of your current color might do the trick.

- Try your new look out on the town. After you get your fashion upgrade or low-key makeover, don't sit in the house. Make plans to go out dancing or have dinner with some friends in a visible location.

Improve Your Attitude

Brooke always seems upbeat. People in her office smile at her when she walks in the door wishing everyone a good morning. On the street, men and women always notice her; she just seems like someone you want to know. Brooke never thought she was stunningly attractive, but she seemed to get more attention than most no matter where she went. She never really knew why, but people seemed to gravitate to her. She just had an attitude based on feeling good and being confident enough to take on the world. Everyone around her definitely believed she could do it!

It's all in the attitude … a good one, anyway. If you want to be looked at differently by other people, you have to command that energy. Carry yourself like someone who gets noticed, and people will start to notice. As mentioned, you don't have to be a supermodel to get attention; you just have to be attractive to others—meaning that you have something that draws or attracts them to you.

Having a positive attitude is *very* attractive. People pick up on your energy. Your level of confidence shines through. When you feel good about yourself, it shows in your walk, your talk, and your overall demeanor. People want to speak to you because you appear more open and friendly. Guys will approach someone who is smiling or appears happy and friendly.

Think about how you appear to others. Do you look like you are carrying the world on your shoulders, or do you appear confident and happy? Shake off your bad thoughts and feel that you have everything under control. Your positive attitude will make people notice.

It's good to remember that you are unique and there are men who will like you for a lot of reasons. When they compliment you, enjoy it. When other women start looking at you wondering who you are, feel good about being you. Every woman has reasons to feel confident and good about herself. Let this confidence shine whether you're in your own private world or interacting with others. Your positivism will definitely rub off on others and make others want to get to know you better.

Make It Happen!

Having a positive attitude will help you keep your confidence level high and make you feel better about yourself.

To get started, follow these steps:

1. On one side of a piece of paper, write down negative thoughts that make you feel unhappy.

2. On the same page, in the same format, write down what you say to yourself when a man you wouldn't normally be attracted to notices you or other people compliment you.

3. Write down next to each negative thought the phrase "I deserve to be happy," or "There is no reason for me to not get what I want."

Don't ...

- Allow negative thoughts. Bad thoughts are going to pop into your head, but let them come and go. Dwelling on something that you cannot change won't help you feel better about it.

- Believe you are not attractive enough to get what you want.

Do ...

- Give yourself positive affirmations every day. Say them when you look at yourself in the mirror. Say them in your head when you feel the "unworthiness" feeling coming on.

- Continue to replace negative thoughts with positive affirmations when you see that men find you attractive.

End the Self-Sabotage

Now that you have successfully begun to master the way to look and act, you need to identify and possibly change the way you interact with men. It sounds silly, but many women complain about not being able to meet nice men—all while avoiding situations where they could meet them. Women often discourage men without realizing it.

Dating is tough, but you don't have to go into combat with every unsuspecting man. Go through these additional training drills to ensure that this will no longer impede your progress.

Melt the Ice Queen

Here's the scenario. You're out with your girlfriends at a dance club. A song you like starts playing and you either sing along or tap your foot along with the music. A guy sees you and cautiously comes up to ask you to dance. You see him out of the corner of your eye and immediately think, "Oh, man, here he comes to ask me to dance." You scan him up and down and a look of irritation creeps across your face. Unsuspectingly, he circles around you for a bit, mustering up his courage. By the time he walks up and opens his mouth, you cut him off saying, "No, I don't want to dance." He is immediately shot down, embarrassed, and slinks away to the corner.

There is a variety of problems here. If you're sending out signals that you want to dance, be prepared for someone to ask. If not, maybe change the signals. Another problem is the message you send. You're totally in the right to say "No," but in doing so, be prepared to be labeled unapproachable. If men see you shoot a guy down before he even gets out of the gate, they will steer clear of you. You are left wondering why men are not approaching you, and thinking that they are jerks. They are thinking that you are an ice queen and that their chances are better somewhere else.

Same scenario, different result: You're out with your girlfriends at a dance club. A song you like plays over the speakers and you're really feeling it. A guy comes up and asks you to dance. You scan him quickly and note that he is not your type. Still, you really like the song and want to get on the dance floor. So you decide to dance with him. You find he's actually a pretty smooth dancer. You end up dancing for a few more songs and then he asks you if you would like something to drink. You sit with him and you are pleasantly surprised to find he is a pretty cool guy. You chat for a while and then go back to your girlfriends. After this experience, you get approached repeatedly by other men asking you to dance.

By being open and just having fun, more men will see you as someone with whom they can have a good time. Remember, you're going out to have fun, so have fun! Don't put up barricades if you don't need to. You don't have to be bothered by people you don't want to deal with, but you're not behind enemy lines, either. Be open enough to interact and let your hair down.

Make It Happen!

Men pay attention to women more than women realize. Don't give them an opportunity to make you a Prisoner of War (POW) before you even get a chance to interact.

Don't ...

- Continue this POW behavior.
- Let your friends encourage the behavior either.

Do ...

- Observe how you interact with men when you are not interested in them. Do a mental check to see if your body language sends a strong signal of "No."
- Watch other women in the same situation. What do they do differently? Is it better or worse?
- Practice saying "No" with a friendly smile.
- Look friendly and approachable regardless of your interest.
- Keep your mood positive to attract others.

I have a friend who always has a sour expression on her face. She always looks great, but men never approach her because she doesn't look like she even wants to be there. I also once had a guy friend who broke up with his girl-friend because every time he saw her she was in a bad mood. She saw him as her boyfriend, someone she could vent to, and even thought he would take this as a compliment. However, he just saw her complaining every time he saw her—instead of smiling and letting him know how glad she was to see him!

Drill Sergeant Says ...

Women aren't always aware of the impact of a negative attitude on men. If a man perceives a woman to look disinterested, speak negatively, or have resistant body language, he probably won't try to interact with her. When you interact with a guy, be aware of the following:

- Disgusted facial impressions
- Body language that implies that you are irritated
- Catty or negative comments about other people
- Critical comments toward him
- Behavior that shows you're not pleased

No one wants to be around someone who can't have a good time. A guy isn't necessarily going to tell you why he doesn't want to be bothered with you, he just won't put up with it. He'll go Missing in Action (MIA) and leave you alone. Take note of how you interact and keep the negative behavior in the brig!

Don't Let Disappointment Disappoint You

Have you ever met one of those women who wears her un-happiness like body armor? Some women show their discon-tentment so heavily that they unconsciously ruin the evening for any man who wants to try to meet them. Let's face it, the dating terrain is tough. You go out and there are 10 women to every man. You may feel every other woman looks better than you and your insecurities start making you nervous. Then you look around and most of the guys are either talk-ing to someone already, are married, or look like losers. Even the strongest women can start to lose heart. You begin to believe that you'll never meet anyone, so you get some-thing to drink and stand around waiting for it all to end.

If you begin to lose faith, your attitude will show to everyone! Don't bomb your evening. It's one thing to not have your expectations met, but another to let that ruin your night out. Meeting men is a dance in which you invite them with receptiveness. If you look bored, disgusted, or fed up, you are sending the message that you might be that way if he approaches you.

Try to look at the redeeming light in any situation. So what if there aren't any men who interest you at the party or club? Seek out a couple of the cool girls and meet them instead. Not in the mood to meet lots of new people? Bring friends you can talk to or people-watch with. And even if you meet a few men that you don't want to date, think of it as an investment in the future. Not only are you getting great practice at your new positive attitude (and maybe your new look), but you're building a reputation as a positive person. You never know—the guy you're impressing but don't want to date may have a great roommate you *would* want to date!

Make It Happen!

If your objective is to meet new people, then don't march them off by not enjoying yourself. Draw more positive experiences to you and you will have more fun in social settings. Don't ...

- Feed into a negative feeling and let your disappointment show.
- Relate those negative feelings with people around you.
- Be openly rude or frustrated—you never know who the person you are being rude to knows in your circle or in general.

Do ...

- Observe your own behavior in a social setting.
- Identify when you're starting to feel anxious and change your attitude to be more positive.
- Take a moment, go to the restroom, and regroup.
- Remind yourself that you're there to have a good time, regardless of what happens.
- Use the opportunity to meet new people!

Getting Yourself Out There

You've done a great job so far, soldier. Now that you feel good about yourself, it's time to let the world know you're ready! It won't help you to enhance yourself if you keep doing the things that keep you from the kind of interactions and relationships you want. Doing the same thing just gets you the same result! It's time to get empowered and prep yourself to get back on the firing line.

You may feel like you're on a journey onto the battlefield alone, but take heart and trust your training, and you'll have success. You just have to put yourself out there. It doesn't matter if you're shy or chatty and engaging. The man you want isn't hiding in the bushes or waiting to storm through your door. Your job is to do everything you can to make him come to you. In other words, create new opportunities.

The Glass Is Half Full

Sometimes when you think about being single, negative images come to mind. If you're single and in your late 20s or older, most of your friends may be married, and, unless you live in a very large city, activities for people your age may revolve around families or younger singles. If you're in your 30s or 40s, you may find that the single women around you are divorced with kids or were never married and are single parents. But typically, anyone who's single has made a choice somewhere down the line.

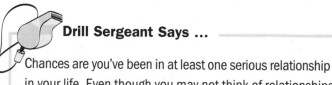

Drill Sergeant Says …

Chances are you've been in at least one serious relationship in your life. Even though you may not think of relationships in terms of choices, think through your past relationships. Did you …

- Know the relationship you were in was not right for you?
- Choose not to be in a bad relationship?
- Want a better lifestyle for your family?
- Want to feel that you didn't settle?
- Want to wait for a more special guy?
- Just need more?

Just because you're single now doesn't mean no one has ever wanted to make a long-term commitment to you. You've probably made some good choices for yourself without even realizing it. Whatever the case, don't get caught up in the "could-have-beens." There are more opportunities out there for you to have another relationship.

There is nothing wrong with wanting to wait for the right person, rather than just settling for anybody. Don't let anyone or anything make you feel bad about your choices. Instead of looking at what you don't have, look at the single life in terms of what you do have. Whether you have been married or not, whether you have children or not, being single *does* have its advantages. The key is to take advantage of what being single really means.

The Freedom of Being Single

Sometimes we complain about being single and forget that we were more unhappy when we were in a relationship with the wrong guy. Even if your stated goal is to eventually be in a secure, committed relationship, you have to embrace the freedom of being on your own. Being single—and dating—is a lot more fun if you appreciate it and make the most of it.

Just as there is a variety of men to choose from, women come from a variety of different circumstances. If you're fun and carefree, there's a man for you. If you have children and want a loving, caring man to join your family, there's a man for you. If you just want to have someone to stay at home with every night, there's a man for you.

Your type of man is out there! Get out there and find him while he's out looking for you. Get past the crippling belief that there are no good men left, or there is not one that is good for you. This is not the time to sit and mope. This is the time to create action and run with your single lifestyle.

The Space You Are In

Go back to your action plan; if you got this far and have done the work, you know that this is about tipping the odds in your favor. What are you currently doing to change your results? Note your answers to the following:

♡ What do you usually do after work?

♡ What do you do on the weekend?

♡ Who do you typically interact with in your spare time?

♡ Do you have any single friends?

♡ How often do you interact with your single friends?

♡ When was the last time you met any single men?

♡ What was the last social activity that you participated in?

♡ When was the last time you went on a date?

♡ How often do you go out to meet new people?

♡ How often do you just say, "It's not worth the effort"?

Look at your answers. Compare them to the profiles that follow. Which one do you fit into?

> A. You're a homebody and really don't have the will or the energy to go out of your way to meet people. You feel that if it takes too much effort, then you would rather not do it. You mostly spend time alone and don't really invite other people in.

B. You do get out there now and then, but you haven't changed the circles of people you interact with. You hang out with friends, but most of them are paired off, married, or parents. Your weekends are full, but you don't meet many new people.

C. You go out on dates, but it's not the stellar experience you thought it should be. You haven't met the guy of your dreams and you would really like to. Unfortunately, you keep meeting the same type of people. You go out to the same places, hoping that Mr. Right will surface, but the more you go out, the more disgusted you feel. The dating scene stinks!

Have you learned anything about yourself that you weren't aware of? Do you fit into one of these profiles, but really don't like what it says about you?

Well, if you're trying to meet the right person to have a great relationship with, you shouldn't *want* to match any of these profiles. You want to strive to match profile D:

D. You're a woman who masters her environment, feels good about herself, is in control of her dating life, and is bound to meet the man she will have a long-term relationship with.

If this is what you want, it's time to do the work.

Sitting at Home Won't Help You

*Alexandra felt that she had a very full life. She had
a great job, great friends, and owned her home.
Alexandra worked from home most nights and ran
her makeup distributor business on the weekends. She
was always on the go, setting appointments, doing
demonstrations, and going to seminars. If Alexandra
had to squeeze one more thing into her calendar, she
would scream! When asked if she was dating anyone,
Alexandra would always say she never meets anyone.
It never dawned on her to make time to do so.*

Have you heard the adage, "Those who get help are those
who help themselves?" That's what this mission is about.
You're not going to meet the man you want by doing what
you've been doing. Most women just aren't that lucky.

Women are skilled creatures. When they don't know
something, they do some research or get guidance. When
they aren't sure where to start, they at least know the people to start with. Women are successful in their careers,
owning property, managing their financial affairs, raising
their children, and taking care of themselves. The one area
most women feel out of control with is dating—or the lack
thereof. Isn't it logical to think that if women can control
so many other things, they could control this area as well?

Now is the time to stop complaining about your love life and start doing things to make it better. You can immediately implement change by getting away from scenarios that are causing you more harm than good. Even if you have obligations to others, start putting your needs first for a change. Make the commitment to take control of your single lifestyle rather than just waiting for something to happen. You are in control of your schedule and your obligations. Make the time that you need to get out and meet people. This might mean just getting off the couch and going to an event to mingle, or it might mean politely declining an invitation that involves only your married friends. Whatever you need to do to make room for your new single lifestyle, make it happen. Once you have opened the door, new opportunities will come your way.

Make It Happen!

Pick out some new activities to get you mixing and mingling. Map out what you want to do and get on it!

Don't ...

- Allow other people to question what you are doing.
- Feel guilty about making this time for yourself.
- Give naysayers too much ammo by telling them what your intentions are.

continues

continued
Do ...

- Get a calendar to block out time for your new "me" project, so you can track how much time you are dedicating to your cause.

- Start by setting aside two weekends a month to do something to get yourself out there.

- If you have kids, set up a play date with friends or a relative, or get a babysitter three or four times a month so you have room to interact with other singles or dating prospects.

- Share your plans (and the results) with understanding friends to build a support network.

- Keep everything in balance so that one area of your life doesn't pull you away.

- Dedicate 80 percent of your spare time for your own pursuits and 20 percent of your time for friends, family, and children's activities.

- Get a partner in crime to go with you to singles events.

Changing Your Routine

Building time into your schedule sounds easy on paper. Following that regimen is more challenging. You're probably already caught up in the routine of going to work, running errands, keeping up your home or apartment, and taking care of the kids, if you have them. Adding time to an already busy schedule may seem impossible, but it has to be done, soldier. If you're not dating and you want to be, then you have to make time to focus on activities that will enhance your single lifestyle.

The following sections suggest ways to change your routine to increase your opportunities to get out and meet new prospects.

Drill Sergeant Says ...

Do not use this extra time to run away from your objective. Use the time for what it was meant for—doing things to help you meet the man that you want!

Enlarge Your Circles

Olivia didn't have any single friends. She socialized only with her married friends and rarely went out to meet new people. Occasionally, one of the married couples would bring a stray man to a barbecue or child's birthday party, but Olivia was always too busy helping with the setup or serving to chitchat. Olivia wasn't happy being single and knew she better do something about it. Her love life was going nowhere fast.

Expanding your network is the most vital thing you can do to enhance your single lifestyle. The more singles you have in your platoon, the more opportunities you will have to meet more people. It's fine if all your friends are married or have significant others, but the more you hang out with them, the less likely you are to meet the men you want to date.

Couples typically hang out with other couples because they can relate to one another, and sometimes single friends and family get pulled in. If you spend most of your time with them, then what are you relating to? Time with them takes away from time you could be interacting with like-minded single people looking for dates!

Make It Happen!

Manage your time so that the bulk of your free time is spent with other singles or on dates.

Don't ...

- Spend your free time with people who have what they want when you don't.

- Let couples convince you to spend all your time hanging out with them.

Do ...

- Spend the bulk of your free time doing things to enhance your single lifestyle.

- Spend time with married or long-term committed friends on occasion.

- Encourage your coupled friends to invite other single people when they have events, if they are willing.

Step Out of the Gymboree

Francine was the favorite aunt to six children. Not having children of her own made it easy for her to host sleepovers or chauffeur the kids to various activities. Francine loved the kids, but sometimes regretted that she never spent time with other adults. Her sisters and brothers depended on her help with babysitting, and she really didn't mind. Sometimes, Francine wanted to accept some of the invitations that her single friends would offer, but she didn't want to disappoint the kids. Francine might as well have had six children of her own!

Another trap that single women fall into is the children trap. Whether taking care of their own kids full-time or hanging out with friends who have kids, this can take you out of the singles scene (except for the few eligible single dads out there!). Between the baby showers, birthdays, and soccer games, you may find yourself always doing something with children.

Sure, it's fun to do sometimes, but you have an objective, and you're not going to meet it at a Saturday-morning soccer game. If there *are* men at these events, they're more than likely husbands and fathers. If you are a parent, aunt, or godparent, some events are important, but not every one.

No one is saying you should never spend time with your or your friends' children. Just find ways to balance that time with your single-adult time. If you want your own significant other, you can't let the children's world dominate your own.

Of course, if you have children of your own, it may be more challenging to carve out time for yourself. Your children come first, and they come with lots of responsibilities and obligations. Find ways to balance your time with theirs. If you are in a shared custody situation, plan some dating time on their dad's weekend. Take advantage of overnights with aunts and uncles or grandparents. Find ways to create your own adult interactions. This is especially important if you don't want to bring people you're dating into your children's lives too soon. Juggle your schedule to accommodate both worlds until you're ready for this next step.

Make It Happen!

Find a way to make time for children's activities and time for your single lifestyle.

Don't ...

- Try to attend every event you're invited to.
- Feel guilty about not attending everything.

- Let your friends, children's father, or family members make you feel guilty.

Do ...

- Be clear on how much time you can give to children's events.
- List the children's activities you're able to attend for a particular month.
- Use your calendar to manage these activities within your goal of sharing 20 percent of your time with others.
- Plan dating activities when your children's father has them.
- Ask a family member to keep the kids overnight.
- Get a babysitter to watch the kids a few nights a month.
- Be strong in your decisions and advocate for yourself.

Meet New People

When people are single for a while, they start to notice that their circles of friends change. Whether through career changes or friends getting married, becoming parents, or moving away, the people you know in your 20s may not be the same as those you know in your 30s. Your fun, single girlfriends might be married and planning to have children.

If you aren't in the same circumstances, this only reinforces the feeling that you are not where you want to be. Instead of feeling bad, you need to call for reinforcements. Expand your ranks and surround yourself with people who have the same goals as you do: interacting with other singles. If you no longer have connections with other single people, it's time to meet new people!

Where do you meet them? Think about where you spend the most time with people. There may be single people at work around your age. If you work out at a gym, more than likely there are people around your age, and you already have something in common with them. What kind of social groups are you involved in? Are there singles you haven't connected with that you could reach out to?

Making the effort to interact with other singles can really pay off. You'll meet new people, then you'll meet people they know, then you'll learn where other people meet, and before you know it, you'll be surrounded with people who have the same goal as you!

Make It Happen!

Continually expand your singles network.

Don't ...

- Expect every single person to be as focused as you are on your goal, but get to know them.

- Limit yourself in the types of people that you meet—be open to meeting people that are not your usual type. For example, if you're the sharp, business type, be open to meeting more creative people.

Do ...

- Make it a goal to meet a new single person at least once a month.

- Leverage meeting new single friends into meeting more single people, especially eligible men.

- Join a singles, networking, or volunteer group that matches your interests.

- Meet other single people in your current world—at work, or through a social or religious activity.

Try a New Bag

If you're at a loss about where to meet these new people you're supposed to be meeting, you may need to try some new places. Think about the last time you really had fun with other people. Was it someplace you'd never been before? Were you following an artistic urge? Were you learning something new? Think about what motivates you and let it guide you to new places and activities.

Don't be intimidated by trying something new! If you are, sign up for a class with a friend or go to an event where you will see some familiar faces. You could also try things on a smaller scale. For instance, instead of going to a big dance-club opening, try an acoustic show at a bookstore or coffeehouse. Trying new things is what life is all about. Before you fell into your current routines, you probably did new things all the time. It's time to get back into that mind-set.

Embrace the chance to do something fun; interact with people who like to have fun and want to meet new people, too. Look around your neighborhood and discover the activities it has to offer. If you live in a large metropolitan city, there are probably a ton of things to do, but it may be hard to find exactly what you are looking for. If you have an idea, surf the Internet for directions to activities that interest you. If you are from a smaller town, start with your local newspaper, community center, or visitor's bureau to generate some new ideas.

If you're still at a loss, here are some great starting points to get you out and meeting people:

Internet Dating
You may have been curious about Internet dating but have never tried it. There are plenty of sites to choose from, such as Match.com or Yahoo. Most allow you to post a picture and profile and view other pictures and profiles from other singles. It's generally easy to get started. All you need is an e-mail address and a recent picture of yourself. You don't even have to post your picture; you can just offer it to people you're interested in after a few e-mail exchanges.

There are a lot of profiles to wade through, so take your time and only interact with those who seem promising. Not everyone is going to be Prince Charming, but there might be some that are close to it. If not, use the site to meet people, make friends, and get some dates.

Singles Calendars

If Internet dating seems too daunting for you, just use the same sites to get information on singles events. Some Internet dating sites coordinate fun activities for singles, such as comedy shows, music nights, cooking classes, dance lessons, and professional networking. Sometimes they even limit the number of men and women attending so that everyone will have someone of the opposite sex to talk to. These events take the pressure off meeting someone for the first time by making the interaction fun and nonintimidating. Even if you don't make an immediate love connection, you're sure to have a good time and meet some new people.

Adult Classes

If you're interested in speaking a new language, doing something artistic, learning to dance, or just getting involved in something creative, why not take a class at your local junior college or community center? You'll meet people with similar interests, with the added benefit that they might actually live in your area! You'll learn something new, have fun, and expand the circle of people you can potentially date.

Gyms

If you're more of an active person, consider joining a gym. It's easy to meet people and the members are usually easy-going. You could swim; take cardio, yoga, or Pilates classes; use cardio and weight machines; or just do your own thing. You'll meet people who enjoy working out and living a healthy lifestyle. Also, you can meet a gym buddy who will help you stay on your program.

Adventure Groups

Maybe you're even more adventurous and regular meet-and-greets really bore you. If you're up for a physical challenge, you could join an adventure club or group that gets together to go hiking, climbing, kayaking, or camping. These groups are usually set up by type of activity, level of experience, and age. Some will even mention if the focus for the group includes meeting other single people. There are formal clubs and informal groups to choose from. Go out and make some new memories in your new adventures!

Singles Groups

These are groups that hold events specifically for singles to meet other singles, from charity events to speed dating. Other activities could include dances, ice cream socials, sporting events, movie nights, and dinner outings. Look for singles groups in your area in your local paper or via the Internet.

Matchmaking Services

If you really want to focus on dating, why not use a match-making service? Some involve you doing the research to find your perfect match, while others offer supremely personalized service where an individual will match you with someone. These services learn and evaluate things about you and match you with someone based on your interests and criteria. Pricing can range based on the level of service you are looking for. Don't feel strange about investigating this possibility. A lot of people successfully find dates this way!

Make It Happen!

Scout out new activities and get ready for a new adventure.

Don't ...

- Try something once and give up because you didn't like one event.
- Be discouraged if you don't meet anybody on your first try at something new.
- Put too much pressure on yourself to do something really adventurous and extremely challenging.

Do ...

- Slate one of these activities for your first day of work on your single lifestyle.

continues

continued

- Slate different activities every two or three weeks so you can explore different activities and groups.
- Look for other activities to fill up your new social calendar.
- Start off with events that seem fun and motivating.
- Be positive and open to people you are meeting.

Create the Scenario You Want

As you build your single lifestyle, meeting people and dating will take on a whole new meaning. No longer will you sit at home waiting for the phone to ring—you'll be out doing things you enjoy. You'll be in control, creating a winning strategy for yourself in what used to look like a bleak environment.

When your energy is up, men will react positively to you and approach you more easily. Even if you don't make love connections right away, you'll be in situations that will help you meet and make connections with people you wouldn't otherwise meet.

You'll also have more balance in your schedule. You'll still have time for married friends or your nephews/nieces, but you'll also have time to be out there interacting with potential dates or people helping you to meet them.

You'll have a lifestyle filled with fun activities, cool people, and more community involvement. You've turned a glass you once thought was half empty into one that's very full and satisfying!

6

Breaking Through the Misconceptions

Before you bought this book, where did you go to meet men? Were you even meeting any? Ask any single woman where she meets men and she'll probably look at you blankly and ask you the same thing.

Let's face it: It's getting more and more difficult to meet men on an everyday basis. Times have really changed. You're probably not sitting around on Saturday nights looking whimsically at your dance card wondering if Jim or Ted would be the better date. In fact, your dance card is probably empty, and Jim and Ted are slamming beers down at Shooters. If you haven't updated your dating philosophies, it's time for an upgrade.

Ideas That We Bought Into

As James Brown once sang, "This is a man's world." Women have fought for equal rights, equal pay, and equal respect. Unfortunately, equality in dating has been overlooked. Women still believe they have to wait on a man to initiate everything.

Imagine a woman who comes to work and tells everyone she proposed to her man. Mouths would drop and she would be the laughingstock of the office. Women just aren't supposed to approach men this way; if they do, society says they're brazen, fast, inappropriate, or loose.

A lot of dating rules are built on women remaining "in their place" and waiting for the man to make the first move. However, depending on the man and the circumstances, you might be waiting a long time. Read on to see why these philosophies won't get you a man any sooner than doing nothing at all.

Following All the Rules

The craze for following rigid dating rules is over. Men who want relationships become just as frustrated trying to find someone nice to date, so they're likely to walk right past someone who shuts them out by following the "rules" too closely.

It's hard enough to connect with people. If you add in a bunch of game playing, you're going to get nowhere fast. Yes, you should maintain some degree of coolness; you don't want to seem desperate. However, if a man gets the idea that you're pushing him off just to do it, he'll decide you're just too much work. Do the men and yourself a favor—just be real, and realize that rules are meant to be broken.

So, what misconceptions are out there? The following sections discuss some common ones.

Being the Lamb Instead of the Lion

"Sugar and spice and everything nice, that's what little girls are made of." If you go by the classic nursery rhyme, the girl who's a big sugar cookie gets the man. Mothers have been shoving this down their daughters' throats for years: men only want to date the pretty thing who doesn't cause problems or make waves. The woman who was a sweet little lamb would always have a man because she was a demure and delicate flower he was proud to have. If she was doting, perfect, and a lady, what man wouldn't want her? Nowadays? A lot of them!

True, some men still have 1950s notions and want you to stay home looking perfect and baking cookies, but more men these days want a real woman and an equal partner. They want you to have a brain and use it; they want you to have opinions; they want you to stand up for yourself and your beliefs. Now men want you to be a lion, not a lamb. They want a strong woman who can help raise strong kids who can deal with modern society.

Drill Sergeant Says ...

The top complaint men have about women today is that they can't seem to find a woman who is real. Men want you to be the person you are and not some picture-perfect icon. Be yourself and you'll get the man you want! Stop hiding who you are. You'll be surprised how many dates you get.

Waiting On Mr. Right

Karen knew that Mr. Right was just around the corner. Many of her friends were married; she had to be next! She didn't really bother dating around because she felt that she would just "know" when she met him. Besides, looking for him wasn't necessary, because he was supposed to find her. She also didn't make any major life decisions, such as buying a house or taking great vacations, because she was supposed to do all that with "him." Karen knew her life was going to be great—just as soon as she met her Mr. Right ....

Waiting on "The One" is no way to live your life. Waiting on Mr. Right is like waiting for a bus on a rainy day—it takes forever, and all the wrong ones come in the meantime. While you're waiting, life is passing you by.

Some people really do believe there's only one Mr. Right, while others believe you'll meet a few of them. Either way, you don't want to be so wrapped up in looking for the ideal man that you either think every man who comes along is him, or try to reshape every man into the ideal you have in your head.

Break the cycle of hoping and waiting for the perfect man to appear. What if you miss him because your antennae thought he couldn't possibly be "The One"? Keep getting out, meeting people, and enjoying the experience.

Don't assume that every guy you meet is "The One" in the making. Meeting different people will expand your horizons. You may not even see "The One" coming because you're having too much fun getting to know him. Let him appear on his own, and enjoy life in the meantime.

Drill Sergeant Says ...

Are you a victim of trying to make Mr. Wrong into Mr. Right? Do you ...

- Keep trying to shove a square peg into a round hole?
- Convince yourself that he's a nice guy and his weird habits will grow on you?
- Tell yourself that he may be your only chance at long-term commitment?
- Secretly pray that he will want the same things you do out of life, even though he says he doesn't?
- Hope that he will eventually grow to like your friends and family?
- Think that you will magically get along all the time?
- Wish that he would become the prince you've always wanted?

continues

continued

If you find yourself relating to these questions, then you need to ...

- Evaluate whether or not you're accepting your guy for who he is. If you're trying to force him into your world and he's not a great fit, then look for someone who is.

- Know what is really important to you. If you don't agree on things such as having children, fidelity, or whether or not you should stay home with the kids, then you have some big mountains to climb. Make sure that you're on the same page.

- Be realistic about who this guy is. If he never likes being social in large groups, maybe he never will. You can't change people, but you can change your expectations. Accept him for who he is, and then ask yourself if you want a long-term commitment.

- See that it is more important to have the right guy than a wrong relationship. It's sometimes hard to be alone, but it's even harder to be in the wrong situation. Find the right person before you make a long-term commitment. More time getting to know him up front will give you less time in a bad relationship.

If It's Meant to Happen, It Will

Darlene did not believe in waiting on a man, nor did she expect every man she met to be "The One."

96

Instead, she believed that if love was meant to happen for her, it would just happen. Darlene worked on the toll bridge on the 11 P.M. to 7 A.M. shift. She would sleep during the day and then watch television until time for work. She worked Saturdays and had one day off during the week. Darlene rarely went out on the weekends because she was generally tired after working on Saturday nights. Still, she thought she would meet her man when the universe made a way for it to happen.

There's nothing wrong with believing in Fate, but you have to give Fate some room in which to work! How are you going to meet people if you never make yourself available?

Sometimes life's obligations keep you from being a party girl and going out every weekend. However, you have to make some time to get out and interact with other people. How do you even know if men are interested in you if they never get a chance to see you?

Dating in this era is all about you putting yourself out there. Stop at the local coffeehouse for a latte before you go home. Grab an early dinner at the local café with live entertainment. Putting yourself out there helps Fate push you into the man you are supposed to be with. Expecting him to fall out of the sky is not going to work.

If you want to have an edge in the new dating scene, then leave the old beliefs in the dust. Dating is just like fashion—changing with the trends can make you a fashion icon, whereas if you don't, you can be a last-season has-been. Try new things, explore a little bit outside your comfort zone, and be open to new possibilities. Your dating life can only get better from here.

Make It Happen

If you want to revamp your dating situation, try something new. Remember to find activities that interest you so you'll stick with them:

- **Volunteer.** Many groups are always looking for a big heart and an extra pair of hands. You'll feel good about what you're doing and meet like-minded people who want to make a difference. Do you already belong to a volunteer organization? Try a new one! You'll meet more people and expand your reach in helping others in your community.

- **Extended education.** Is there a class you've been long-ing to take, or an educational interest that you let fall by the wayside? Find a class at your local community college or university extension program. You'll learn something new and make new friends in class and around campus.

- **Sports.** You don't have to only be active through a gym. You can meet new people on the golf course, on an intramural team, or through a local league. Be active and meet other people for fun on the field and off.

- **Hobby groups.** Are there other hobbies that interest you? People form groups for art appreciation, travel, crafts, music, and other activities. Get into a group and find a network of new people.

- **Artistic endeavors.** If you'd like to be involved in the arts, but don't consider yourself the artistic type, get involved behind the scenes. Shakespeare festivals, independent art shows, and community theaters are always looking for support. You can help fund-raise, create signage, or scout for stage materials. Not only will your help support a production, you'll see the fruits of your labor and meet more people.

Keep your interests open and new opportunities will come your way!

The Longer You Wait, the Harder It Will Be

Unlike a lot of the women in her family, Jody didn't marry early. She always wanted to be a judge, so education became her Number One priority. While many of her friends were getting engaged, Jody was preparing for her law exams. While her friends were having babies, Jody was working for a judge that she would one day replace. Even when Jody's mother would invite a surprise blind date to Sunday dinner, Jody would be polite but excuse herself and go home before dessert. Jody stuck to her guns and eventually

became a Superior Court judge in her county. She worked long hours and didn't make time to date. However, she did make time to speak at the law offices on various college campuses and at various law association meetings. At one of her campus visits, she met another judge named Jeff. Jody and Jeff clicked and immediately started dating. They are now married and expecting a baby.

At one time, a woman's entire focus after high school was to meet the right man so she could become a great wife. Nowadays, a woman can be a great wife, wonderful mother, and an electrical engineer. Many women put a priority on their careers, but that doesn't mean that they don't want to have a family as well. Even though some women are very career-focused, they still have great opportunities to meet Mr. Right. It's not necessarily harder, it just takes more effort to get yourself out there.

You can have your career and still make time to socialize—even if it is with people in your professional field. The more time you spend socially mixing, the better your chances are to meet other people. The connections you make could not only help you further your career, they could also lead you to someone you'd like to know on a deeper level. If your career has taken priority up to now, make your connections with others a priority as well.

The Good Ones Are All Taken

As the expression goes, you can't believe everything you hear. If all of the good ones are taken, then why are there good men complaining about not being able to find a good woman? Unfortunately, the good men and the good women don't easily find each other. A lot of times they're distracted by either the wrong people or their friends who are discouraging them.

Don't let this happen. There are great guys out there—you just have to be *out there* to meet them. When you date, you're going to meet some people whom you don't want to be with long-term. That is the beauty of dating. The more you do, the more you will learn to hone in on exactly what you are looking for. Keep believing that the right one is out there for you, and you will meet him.

A New Age

To keep up with the changing dating scene, you have to change with it. The biggest change probably needs to happen with your attitude. It's easy to sit back and say that dating is too hard. You can be as successful as you would like to be if you accept the fact that things are different, so a different course of action is necessary.

Learn how to deal with this new dating environment and find new dating tools to use. Embrace change and take advantage of your training. If you do, you will only get better at navigating through what was once a tough environment.

Date with Intent

Suzette and Tammy had been friends for years. In their circle of friends, they were the only ones who had never been married or had children, so they hung out a lot. Suzette wanted to get married, but the men she met didn't seem to want that level of commitment. Suzette would still date them and eventually find herself falling for them, but these relationships would usually fall apart, and once again Suzette would find herself lonely on Saturday night.

Tammy also wanted to get married, but she only dated men who seemed to want what she wanted. Tammy had seen the disappointment Suzette constantly encountered and crafted her dating style differently. Tammy began to date with intent—she only dated men who eventually wanted a long-term commitment. Asking early on what a man was looking for helped her to weed out the men who were only looking for a party girl. Tammy cut men off early who didn't fit her profile, so she never wasted her time. Instead, she spent her time getting to know the men who were looking for more.

One new perspective is that you are no longer just waiting for a date to happen. Whether you're dating to have fun and meet new people or dating to meet someone special, it's important to date with intent. You are in control of what you want your end result to be, so set your goals before you even get out there.

People are more successful when they have a plan. Having a plan keeps you focused on what you really want. Get ready, you will have an opportunity to flesh out your plan more in the next chapter.

Go Get Him!

There's a lot of truth in saying that the man you want is not going to ring your doorbell anytime soon. You're going to have to go out and get him. You don't have to feel like you're on a manhunt, but you do have to at least go and see where he might be hanging out. With the multitude of Internet dating sites popping up daily, it's easy to see that people are finding it harder and harder to meet. Whether you meet him online or out in the world, make the effort to meet him or put yourself in the position so he can meet you.

Take Your Power Back

Times have changed, and it's up to you to change with them. No one is making you a victim but you. Yes, it's challenging to meet men. However, no one is saying that you have to sit at home without them. Be empowered and put the effort where it needs to be—working on how you are going to get the dates that you want, rather than complaining about not having them. The dates are out there, you just have to be out there in order to get them. Take back your position of power and go out and get those dates!

Make It Happen!

Do you find yourself sitting at home complaining about the dates you don't have, the fun you are not enjoying, or the relationship that is not happening? Change your perspective and look at what you can do instead:

- Make a list of all of the places you want to go but haven't yet.

- Note all of the things you want to try but have been too scared (for example, speed-dating, attending a singles mixer, and so on).

- If you find yourself on the phone with the same girl-friend on nights you want to go out, change it up. Meet her for dinner or drinks instead.

- Need some new scenery? Plan a girl's weekend in a fun city like Las Vegas, Atlantic City, or the nearest happening city near you. You can let your hair down and meet some new people from out of town—or surprisingly enough, from your own hometown.

Get your calendar out and plan some fun activities. Make arrangements with friends for at least two planned events per month. The more you commit, the more concrete your activities will be.

7

Getting What You Want

When they arrive at boot camp, recruits leave their civilian life on the bus. They are reborn into military life by changing their hair, dress, name, and status. New soldiers then follow the military approach to problem-solving, building combat strategies and thinking like a soldier. Like those boot camp recruits, you must get ready to become the professionally trained dating soldier that you are.

In the previous chapters, you focused on things that you could change or enhance about yourself. Now it's time to focus on getting the relationship you've been seeking. Your training can help you refine your dating scenarios so you can know what type of relationship you want and figure out how to get it. Your action plan will help you get specific about what's important to you in a relationship and how to meet men who want what you do. Once you identify your needs, your action plan will help you obtain it. If you're already on the relationship path but feel that you're not getting the relationship you want, your action plan will help you identify trouble areas to help you get your relationship moving along.

Completing Checkpoints on Your Action Plan

The first part of your action plan (see Chapter 3) helped you identify the obstacles in the way of your pursuing a relationship. The second part of your action plan is about clarifying exactly what you want.

By now you should have a good handle on what makes you the person you are, so you should also know what kind of relationship is a good fit for you. Take the time to identify exactly what you need for the relationship you are pursuing.

Specify

Identify in each section what you are looking for. Be as honest as you can, as this part of the plan will help you determine what you truly want.

1. What kind of relationship are you looking for?

   ☐ A committed long-term relationship for companionship

   ☐ A casual long-term relationship—you have a steady guy but you're open to meeting other people

   ☐ A see-ya-when-I-see-ya, casual relationship (on your terms), where you see him only when you want to

   ☐ A committed long-term relationship with marriage as the end result

   ☐ A long-term dating situation with no end commitment

2. What are the most important things you need from this relationship?

♡ Comfort   ♡ Adventure

♡ Support   ♡ Love

♡ Companionship   ♡ Acceptance

♡ Trust   ♡ Stability

♡ Security   ♡ Friendship

Empower

Note what you need to do differently to pursue what you want. Empower yourself by shutting down negativity and turning it into positive support.

3. Replace negative thoughts.

Instead of thinking about negative things that have been said about you, you will think about the following:

_____

_____

_____

_____

107

4. Celebrate your qualities/characteristics.

List the top five things you like about yourself that you want the next man in your life to recognize:

1. _____

2. _____

3. _____

4. _____

5. _____

5. Identify the people who are not helping you in pursuing the relationship you want:

_____

_____

_____

_____

6. How are you going to deal with no longer accepting their negative influence?

_____

_____

_____

_____

Now that you have completed the next part of your action plan, take a moment to seriously review your answers. Are you currently pursuing the kind of relationship that you say you want? Are you still letting other people influence your choices? Use your action plan and the tips in this chapter to help you achieve the kind of relationship you want.

Realize Your Worth

In boot camp, the way to build a better soldier is to understand where the soldier is coming from. The Drill Sergeant can usually tap right into the pain that keeps the recruit stifled from succeeding. The recruit is usually broken down and has to learn to not listen to negative comments that make her feel discouraged. Once the recruit pushes through the negativity (usually being shouted by the Drill Sergeant), she is strong enough to know that nothing and no one can hold her back any longer.

In a similar fashion, women who are not getting the relationships they want typically have negative things to say about relationships, men, dating, and even marriage. These women could be our mothers, sisters, or best friends, but their experience does not have to be ours. Listen to your loved ones, but filter what they are saying.

Focus on things that make you feel good about you. If you do that, then you will be able to take your new tools and get out there and find what you want. Recognize the key that everyone seems to forget after getting kicked around by their relationships: working on themselves.

Make It Happen!

If you're involved in a relationship and It doesn't work out, realize that it happens. Everyone gets hurt. How you deal with your hurt and move on makes a big difference. After you go through a breakup, rebuild yourself by focusing on things that will make things better the next time around.

Think about these things:

- What made your last relationship fail? Can you pinpoint an actual moment or situation that contributed?

- Note things that you would like to do better in your next relationship, such as communicating with your partner more, being more open about yourself, or being more realistic about your expectations.

- Understand that your next relationship doesn't have to end this same way.

- Realize that your last relationship was an isolated situation and is not indicative of every relationship you're going to have.

- Give your next relationship a chance by not bringing past relationship baggage into it.

- Believe that your next relationship will be better than the last.

- Try to keep conversations about your relationship to a minimum when you are speaking to people who are not supportive.

- Don't let others' negativity spoil your happiness.

Feel Good About Who You Are

Monica decided that she was going to do everything she could to increase her advantages in dating. After her relationship with Derrick, she realized that she really didn't feel good about herself. Monica got into a pattern of coming home, sitting on the sofa, and watching hours of mindless television while eating a pint of ice cream. What was the point of keeping up her workout routine if she was just going to keep attracting guys like him? In bed, Monica would run the tape over and over in her head about why Derrick decided he could not have a relationship with her anymore and broke things off. One night, Monica realized that everything that Derrick said was about what was making him unhappy. What about what was making her unhappy? Monica thought about what made her feel bad about herself, and recognized that Derrick couldn't give her what she needed anyway. She decided it was time to get off the sofa and start doing something good for herself.

To get past the negativity, you have to realize that it serves no purpose except to make you feel bad about yourself. Other people can easily point a finger at you and your flaws. Then you start compounding the situation by feeling bad on your own.

It's much better to be more mature and take an inventory of what *you* might have done wrong. The first step is to not wallow in self-pity, guilt, or misguided blame. The sooner you feel better about you, the sooner you can meet the kind of man who enjoys who you are. If some man you dated pointed out your faults—so what? Everybody has them. You can't feel bad about someone not liking something about you; he is only one person. You have to like you—all of you: the good, bad, and ugly parts. The sooner you accept yourself and feel okay with who you are, the sooner you can meet someone who is a better fit.

Drill Sergeant Says ...

How are you going to get what you want in the present if you are hung up on the past? Let negative comments go in one ear and out the other, whether they were said five years ago or five minutes ago. What matters now is your own perception of who you are. A new guy won't know what you did or know what was said in the past. All he will see is that you're a cool woman he wants to spend time with. Be more positive, and leave the past in the past.

Make It Happen!

Let it go! Stop allowing negative stuff to keep you from moving on. Following are some tips:

Don't ...

- Worry about not getting a man because of things that were said about you in the past. Instead of worrying, go out and meet new men. Go to a singles mixer, join a gym, or get a blind date through a friend.

- Put more energy into negative thinking as it is tearing away at your self-esteem. Stop going through the same training drills. If you heard it the first time, you don't need to keep hearing it. Get it out of your head; say positive affirmations instead.

Do ...

- Let go of the negative things people have said about you; realize that negative comments don't define who you are. Celebrate the things that others like about you.

- Make a list of things that men say they like about you. Review the list when you are going out to meet people and make sure these characteristics shine!

- Take inventory of the positive things about you and the qualities that make you unique. Put this list on your bathroom mirror and review it every day.

- Replace negative thinking by reinforcing positive thoughts, words, or phrases about yourself.

Know What You Have to Offer

Every woman has something uniquely different to offer. It can be physical, such as an attractive chest or very fit body. It can be a characteristic, such as the way she laughs or the intensity of her eyes when she is thinking. It can be her quiet nature, or her ability to liven up a room. Whatever your unique, *je ne sais quoi* ability, you need to recognize and celebrate it.

Too many times relationships end and women reflect on the bad times. Instead, think about what made this man fall for you in the first place. The key is to know what you have to offer: the unique person you are and the qualities you bring to the relationship. If you don't know your worth, the men you meet won't either.

Make It Happen!

It's time to realize how great you are! If other men thought you were great in the past, new ones will, too. Show them what makes you you!

Don't ...

- Get stuck thinking about your failed relationships.

- Worry about what you are not, but focus more on who you are.

Do ...

- Know what value you bring to the relationship table.

- Make a list of all of the qualities and characteristics that you bring to a relationship.

- Think about what kind of man would appreciate these attributes.

- Begin to formulate what kind of man would balance your character traits in your next relationship.

Learning How Not to Accept Less

A lot of men consider Irene a good catch. In her late 20s, Irene has a good profession as a nurse, owns her own house, and keeps herself physically fit. The only problem that Irene seems to have is meeting the right type of men to date. She meets all types of men, but instead of dating men who are on her level intellectually or financially, Irene tends to date men who don't have it together, men who are "in between" jobs, or starving artists who end up living off of her. Unfortunately, she thinks these are the only kinds of men who are interested in her.

Another component of realizing your worth is not accepting less than you deserve. If you know that you are a good woman and you deserve a man cut from the same cloth, don't settle for less. In a lot of cases, women end up dating whoever comes their way just because they're not meeting the kind of men they'd *like* to meet.

Review your action plan: What characteristics are you looking for? Are you meeting men who have the same interests as you? Do they have the caring qualities that you need? Are they responsible and supportive? Make sure you're meeting people you really want to date; only you can determine when you're not. Don't settle for anything outside your core criteria.

Make It Happen!

Leverage your action plan to hone in on the kind of man you want to meet.

Don't ...

- Get caught up thinking you can overlook things that are important to you just to have a man.
- Justify accepting less than you should by believing this is your only chance to have someone.

Do ...

- Keep a clear focus on what you need from the potential man you would like to date.
- Remember that you deserve the best and you don't need to settle to have a man.
- Identify the deal-breakers for you when you meet a man to date.

- Establish a minimum standard of what you are willing to accept from a man who wants to be with you (for example, a certain professional or educational level).

Be Sure of What You Want ... and What You Don't

There is a lot of truth in the saying, "Be careful what you wish for, because you just might get it." You have to *know* what you want to *get* what you want. Women may know they want a relationship, but are they really clear on what they want and what they don't? In most cases, no, because they date the next attractive guy who comes along.

Your thinking should be set on what you want in a man and your relationship rather than just accepting what comes. You have more power here than you think! The more specific you are about what you want, the sharper your ability will be to separate who you really want from the riffraff.

If You Want One, Get One

Dana was ready to have a relationship with someone special. She was happy in her life and wasn't lonely, but she was done being alone. Most of her friends were married, and the few single friends she had seemed jaded and frustrated. They even told Dana she shouldn't even try to find a relationship—all men were lousy anyway. Hanging out with her negative friends wasn't

getting her any closer to the relationship she wanted, so Dana spent less time with her complaining friends and more time pursuing the relationship she was after. Dana put a plan together and focused on meeting new female friends to hang out with, making time to go someplace new with them every week. She kept to her action plan and only dated men that met her criteria. Dana is now in a long-term relationship with a great guy she met at a wine tasting party.

There's nothing wrong with taking a stand for what you want. Identify and pursue the relationship you want! You may have been disappointed by how difficult it is to meet desirable men, felt the frustration of not easily connecting with people, and heard the faint ticking of your biological clock. Don't let the pressure get to you. A lot of single men are just as frustrated.

Meeting the right person is always hard, so there is a lot of disconnecting and frustration. Your mission is to put yourself in the best position to meet the right person for you. Of course, you need to do your work: Look your best, feel your best, and meet that someone new with a positive outlook. Get rid of your baggage, anger, hurt feelings, and negative thoughts so they don't become obstacles in your new relationships.

If you want a relationship, then pursue it. Being confidant, going to the right venues, and meeting the right people will remove some of the obstacles that have been in your way.

8

New Tools, New Attitude

In order to win the war, you have to go into battle like a leader, not a follower. Too often women sit on the sidelines waiting for something to change. On the new dating battlefield, you have to be the leader and change your perspective. You have to make things happen.

By looking at dating differently, you can actually have fun, and when you utilize new tools, you can meet more people, feel good, and enjoy yourself. Let the lion come out of you and become more empowered with your dating strategies.

In boot camp, you learn a variety of new skills and work with ever-changing technology. Boot camp trains a soldier to be prepared for the unexpected. At any moment, an enemy can deploy new weaponry or a sneak attack. In Dating Boot Camp, you will also learn to deal with the unexpected. Armed with your action plan and new field strategies, you will navigate your way through the new dating terrain.

What We Learn from Guys

In the field, it is important to gain a competitive advantage. Understanding how other military operatives work helps soldiers in any interrogation situation. In Dating Boot Camp, you can gain insight about men directly from them.

Yes, it's true: Men and women are truly different creatures. Women are socialized differently from the beginning. Growing up, a woman is taught to be a lady-in-waiting— waiting on the perfect man to pick her from the rest of the crowd. On the other hand, men are taught to do the picking, and they don't pick just one woman initially—they pick as many as they can. Then, when they have had enough fun, they select the right woman to marry and have a family.

It is high time that women adopted this philosophy. Being a lady-in-waiting doesn't always get you what you want. Arm yourself with the attitude that you can get what you want by believing it's out there and going after it. Use some of the techniques that men follow to get more quickly to the man you want, *and* have more fun before you're off the market.

Date More Than One at a Time

Elizabeth was married for 15 years. She had been with Keith for at least 20 years, and never had the opportunity to date anyone else. After her divorce, she had some time alone. When she was ready, she went on a date. It felt good to meet other men who thought she was great. Eventually, Elizabeth found herself

going out with three different guys at one time. She had never felt so free! She didn't feel bad about it because she knew she wasn't ready to be in a relationship, especially with the wrong person. She felt it would be clear when the right man made his appearance. In the meantime, she was having fun.

If you feel alarmed by the thought of dating more than one man at once, the first question you should ask yourself is "Why?" You're not committed to anyone. You're not being held to somebody else's standards. There's nothing wrong with exploring your options. Dating is simply that: dating. It doesn't mean you have to deceive anyone or be a player. It means you can meet different people, spend time with them doing things you enjoy, and potentially see them again.

Think about it. Most men don't commit to one woman until they feel pretty certain she'll be a good fit. However, most women meet a "nice" guy and start dating him exclusively. Do you *really* know that he's a nice guy? Do you know everything you should know before you start fantasizing about getting married with the 2.5 kids and the SUV? Probably not.

A man might be leaning toward you as an ideal selection, but he's still going to ride out quite a few more dates before he relinquishes Alison and Carrie. Before you feel shocked, realize that men have been doing this for years. Now it's your turn to be a field operative until you find exactly what you are looking for. In your action plan, you outlined the kind of relationship you're truly seeking. By dating more men, meeting different people, and not getting serious until you find what you want, you will have a better chance of finding that relationship.

Make It Happen!

Date more than one man without committing, and keep yourself out there.

Don't ...

- Talk yourself into believing that you're doing something wrong. You're just turning the tables and doing what men do.
- Listen to dating naysayers and cater your dating practices to what is more socially acceptable.

Do ...

- Feel comfortable enough to interact with more than one man and go out on different dates.
- Begin making dates with the different people you meet.
- Take your time learning to date more than one man at a time if you need to. If this is a totally new concept for you, date two and see how it goes.
- Overbook your calendar!
- Get to know all of the men who ask you out!

To make your new dating practice work, set some ground rules. Think of yourself as a member of a dating special ops force. You can interact, but you can't give away too much information about your assignment until you need to. Here are some rules and guidelines that can help:

1. Go on at least one date with every guy who asks you.

2. Be impartial on making assessments about each guy until you've had a second date with each one.

3. Make notes on each one in a small notebook, such as his likes and dislikes, and things you like about him. Remember to not get them confused.

4. Keep the intimacy to a minimum. Sex can complicate the situation, so it might be best to leave it out of the formula until you feel comfortable enough to scale down your options.

5. Be honest and let your dates know that you are "just dating" until you are ready for a commitment. You can be more forthright and let them know you are seeing other people.

6. Try to pick date locations that will keep you from running into any of your other dates.

7. Don't invite any of them to your home until you're closer to deciding who might be a more long-term fit.

8. Try to keep your dates on the same schedule—if you have had a second date with one, then have a second date with all of them.

9. If you're looking for a serious relationship, only you can determine when you're ready to focus on one guy. Keep your options open until you feel certain.

10. Women openly dating more than one man is a new concept for both men and women. Men might take a while to get used to it, but don't let that smother you.

Don't Let Him Go Too Soon

Vivian enjoyed dating and meeting a variety of people. She found herself starting to favor two particular men out of her dating circle, but couldn't decide which one she liked more: Ben was a free-spirited gym trainer, while Larry was a marketing manager and a serious go-getter. Vivian decided to do something she had never done before: She continued dating both of them until one of them stepped up. Eventually, Vivian grew tired of Ben's wishy-washy behavior and eliminated him from the running. Vivian and Larry are now engaged!

To women who are not used to dating more than one man, the concept initially feels foreign. As you go out with more than one, you might find it easier to gravitate to one man and want to get rid of the others. Don't be too quick to do this! Deciding too quickly defeats the whole purpose of taking your time to date, meet others, and see what appeals to you.

Look at how a man handles a similar situation. If a man decides to date, he sets out to meet as many women as he can. Further, he typically has no problem dating more than one woman at a time. If he starts to favor one woman, he doesn't necessarily halt his efforts with the others. Instead, he becomes more available to the one he favors and a little more distant with the others. He doesn't get rid of all of the women he dates; he just doesn't make as many dates with them. The idea is to be available for the one he wants, while keeping his foot in the door with the others in case things don't work out. It might sound unfair, but this type of dating man is looking out for himself; he wants to give himself as many options as possible before he commits. You can't be mad at him unless he's lying to anyone involved. If he isn't making any commitments to anyone, then he's really doing nothing wrong.

When men play the field, a lot of them will have sexual affairs with all of the women involved. Usually, the women don't know that the man is seeing other women, much less sleeping with them. However, dating doesn't necessarily mean you're having casual sex. You can date different men and not be sexually involved. If you do decide you want to have sex, definitely protect yourself. Also, if you do get involved this deeply, you may want to scale down how many people you are sexually involved with. People get more invested in relationships when an intimate element is introduced.

Now most women will tell you that they don't believe
there are *any* good men out there, so how many women
are really going to have a shot at dating Prince Charming
No. 1 *and* Prince Charming No. 2?

Okay, maybe it's not likely, but you might find yourself
dating two or three nice guys. You might even find that
you like them for different reasons. Take the time to really
see each one for who he is, determine what traits appeal to
you, and get to know each one individually. The one you
want will be even more obvious if he's able to outshine the
other two. When you know which man is a better fit for
you, and you both are interested in a relationship, call it
quits with the other men involved.

Drill Sergeant Says ...

When you are dating more than one man and one of them
seems to outshine the others, don't stop everything and
date only him. Instead, ride it out. More than likely, you
won't have to make a choice—the men who aren't up to par
will eliminate themselves.

Remember the Rules of the Game

When you date more than one guy, you want to maintain a
certain level of dating etiquette. Some of the same rules
apply in other dating situations. Pay attention and adhere
to the guidelines:

♡ If you're dating a guy who has a friend who may be interested in you, you may want to steer clear. You don't want to have a messy dating circle on your hands, especially if you end up dating one of them long-term.

♡ Don't assume because you're dating more than one guy that your girlfriend's guys are up for grabs.

♡ Try to date people who are not in the same circles. You don't want too many people knowing your dating business.

♡ Treat every date with the same courtesy and respect. You don't have to flaunt your other dating experiences in his face.

♡ Don't spend your date talking about your multiple dating challenges. Keep your focus and enjoy the date you are currently on.

Make It Happen!

When dating more than one guy, take your time to get to know them all well before you make any final decisions. Don't ...

- Stop seeing the other men too quickly if you begin to like one in particular.
- Worry about being in a situation where you will have to choose; some men will eliminate themselves without your help.

continues

continued

Do ...

- Date whoever you want, no matter how many different men interest you.

- Keep your options open.

- Have fun getting to know all of the different people you date.

- Pay attention to why you like certain things about each guy.

- Date your options long enough to determine which one is the better fit for you.

Date Just to Date

Lucy had recently ended a long-term relationship. She was used to being with one man and hadn't really had the experience of "playing the field." Newly single, she wanted to see what it felt like to just go out and meet different people. She wasn't sure what she was looking for, but enjoyed being open to meeting people whenever she went out.

Another thing that men tend to do differently from women is to date just for the sake of doing it. Men who aren't sure what they want get out and meet women. If getting out there turns into something more, they then proceed to date. If not, there's no harm, since they didn't make obligations to anyone, so they don't feel bad about it.

Even if you want a serious relationship, sometimes you need to date just to experience the potential relationships that are out there. If you haven't dated in a while, you might find a different environment than there used to be.

Will you be able to find what you are looking for? How will you know if you don't get out there? Take advantage of this great opportunity to get out, meet different people, and explore.

Make It Happen!

Take the pressure off and enjoy dating just for the fun of it. Don't ...

- Get hung up on trying to find the perfect relationship with every date.
- Miss out on the opportunity to date just to date.

Do ...

- Get out and just date!
- If you don't know what you are looking for, then explore.
- Meet different types of people and see what appeals to you.
- Meet people just for the sake of meeting people—the more people you meet, the better the odds you will find more of what you like.

Apply What Works/Discard What Doesn't

In your new dating lifestyle, it is important to continue to use the tools that work for you and discard the old habits and attitudes that were holding you back. In Dating Boot Camp, you will learn how to work with a variety of equipment, but you will have expertise using some more than others. Your new dating tactics may still feel a little different and weird, but the more you replace old habits with ones that work better, the happier you will be.

As you try new techniques such as dating more than one guy at a time, you will see which tactics work better for you. Even though you can drive a tank, you don't always need to. Decide which dating tools you like and which are more challenging.

Put the Word Out

If you're looking for something and are having a hard time finding it, you usually tell other people to keep an eye out for you. You'd probably tell your friends if you were looking for a job, a house, a day-care center, or even a new city to live in. You might ask people their opinion and consider their advice.

Feel free to do the same thing regarding your dating pursuits. Tell your friends you're dating and are open to meeting other people. You never know who knows who, and your friends probably meet eligible people all of the time. Your friends may meet someone single and nice and forget to mention it because it didn't come up in conversation. Keep your dating lifestyle at the top of the minds of those in your inner circles. You may be surprised who they know.

Don't Commit Too Soon

Whether you're dating just to date or looking for something more, date without committing yourself too soon. Rushing into a new relationship with the first nice guy you meet is not going to help you get closer to what you are looking for. You need some time to get to know these guys you're dating—and yourself. Be prepared for this new dating lifestyle to take off—and while you may feel that you've met Mr. Right on the first (or second or third) try, you probably haven't.

Put Your Action Plan into Effect

If you know what you want, don't waste your time when you're not getting it. Too often women will try to "hang in there," hoping that men will change or start treating them better. If a man isn't giving you what you want, move on. In boot camp, you have limited time to do certain tasks. In the morning, you have to get up and be fully dressed for inspection in a matter of minutes. There is no time to waste. You should treat your dating time just as valuably.

Review your action plan. You have mapped out exactly what you want. Are you dating men who want the same type of relationship that you do? Are you meeting men who match your top five most important characteristics? If not, it is time to reassess. Spend your time interacting with men who want what you do. Do not waste your time on people who are not meeting your criteria.

Never Let Him See You Sweat
Always be prepared to meet the man you have been seeking. Women spend a lot of energy complaining about how long they have to wait for the man of their dreams, but when he magically appears, a lot of women aren't ready for him.

If you're out living your life and having fun, you should be ready for him. In boot camp, a deployment can happen at any time, ready or not. Similarly, you could run into the man you have been looking for at any moment. He usually appears when you least expect it. In social settings, have your get-to-know-you questions ready. When you're out, always look your best; wear flattering outfits and look friendly and inviting. Be prepared—he could spring up on you from anywhere!

Meet Men Everywhere You Go

Where are the men? That is the most common question that women who want to meet men ask. The answer is that the men you want are all around you every day. The question is, how open are you to interacting with them?

Think about your daily routine. How many men do you interact with? How do you interact with them? Men say that they find it just as tough to meet nice women. If a man sees a nice woman, he sometimes finds it difficult to speak to her if he cannot read the signs of interest. Men are fearful of being shut down and avoid it at all costs. If you make it easier for a man to interact, there's a greater chance that he will engage.

Let's say you're sitting in a café having coffee. A nice-looking man comes in, orders, and sits near you. He might be interested in you, but he needs to see your interest. If you look up at him and flirt with your eyes, or smile directly at him, or even say hello, he'll know you're interested. Knowing that you're interested, he comes up and asks if he can sit at your table. Make it easier for a man to approach you. Look friendly, laugh, flirt, or even invite him over to sit with you. The more approachable you are, the less intimidated men will be.

Get the Party Started
In your new empowered role, men might approach you or you might want to approach a man. There's nothing wrong with a woman approaching a man first. A lot of men actually appreciate it when they notice a woman and she has the courage to approach them first. Sometimes a man might notice you and not really know what to say. If he is unsure of himself, he might want to speak to you but will allow

the opportunity to pass because he doesn't know how to strike up a conversation. Help him out by striking it up first.

Make It Happen!

If you notice him noticing you but he appears to be shy, take the initiative. Go over to him and strike up a conversation. If he's interested, you have just made it easier for him to interact with you. If he's not, chalk it up to just chatting and move on. When you see an opportunity, don't be afraid to take the lead. Here are some easy conversation starters:

- At a social mixer, go right up and introduce yourself. Follow up by asking him specific questions about the function (how well he is enjoying it, how long he has been there, etc.).

- At a café, either ask him what's the best thing to order, or if he already has, ask him what he got.

- At a professional function, walk up to him, give him your card, and introduce yourself.

- At a bank, post office, or license branch, make a comment about how long the line is and see if he bites.

- At a cocktail party or get-together, say hello and ask him whom he is a guest of. You can then mention who invited you—you may be able to make a quick connection.

Drill Sergeant Says ...

Guys sometimes want to talk to you and don't know what to say. Throw them a bone and help them out. If you feel pretty certain that a guy is interested in you, give him a minor conversation lead-in. It could be anything from "I like your shirt" to "You look like you could use a friend." Being playful and friendly will ease the tension and open a pathway for him to reach out to you. If he is interested, he will catch it!

Be Open

If you're in an elevator and a man starts a conversation with you, what do you do? Do you scowl at him as if to say, "Leave me alone"? Or do you engage in a brief and friendly conversation?

Be open to these moments and see them as opportunities. A quick chat can turn into dinner and drinks if you play your cards right. Men like women who are friendly and look like they want to talk. If you're walking around looking like you don't want to be bothered, believe me, you won't! In fact, he won't say anything at all to you. Don't get passed over. Look friendly and inviting. Try smiling! If a man looks interested, be open to a conversation with him. The more men pick up on you being open, the more they will want to approach you.

Don't Discard Him: Recycle Him as Your Friend

You're going to meet a lot of men in your new dating life-style. Unfortunately, not all of them are going to be the perfect fit for you. Instead of cutting off all ties with them, keep them around as friends. You see, most men just happen to have a lot of *male friends*, and it's just possible that some of these friends will be men you might like to know better.

Having a good male friend can also put you in situations you couldn't access as easily with a girlfriend. For instance, if you're hanging out at a sports bar with a girlfriend, you may look like you're, well, trying to pick up men. If you're with a male friend, you're just hanging out with the guys. Utilize the connection you have made and let your new male friend help you make some more male friends.

Remain in Control

You now have a number of tools to use in your dating strategies. Some of the tips may be easy to use, while others may nudge you out of your comfort zone. Try different techniques and push yourself to do things that you would not normally do.

Whatever you do, keep your situation under control at all times. You are the one directing how involved you want to be, how much disclosure you want to give the men you are dating, and how active you would like to be in your dating practices. Don't let the men you are dating influence you to fall into your past behaviors. Keep applying your new skills until you gain the type of relationship you want.

Don't Let One Man Pressure You

Be careful: Men may have used a lot of the techniques mentioned in this chapter, but they may not want you to. Men are a little "man-selfish," meaning that it's fine if they do something, but it doesn't mean they think that you should. If a man is aware that you are now the empowered dater, he may try to convince you that it is not a great idea to be that way.

Don't let a man pressure you out of doing something you feel good about. Too many times women throw themselves under a bus trying to change things for a man. Don't let a man's insecurity stop you from enjoying yourself. A man might try to convince you that you don't need to date others now that the two of you have met. He might try to monopolize all of your time to keep you from going out with other people. Do not let this happen. If he tries to pressure you to not see other people, then maybe you don't want to see him.

Let him know that you're just getting to know people and haven't committed to anyone yet. Hopefully, he will take a cue from this and just work harder at being the person you want to spend time with. If not, there are more people to meet!

Don't Get Distracted from What You Want

You now know what type of man you want to have in your life. You may meet this man right away or it may take some time. In the meantime, you will meet a lot of people—some who are your "type" and others who aren't. You may even meet men whom you *know* are not the right type for you. For instance, you might like the creative, artsy type, but you know they're not usually a good fit for you in the long run.

Women tend to go after the same type of men whether they're good for them or not. If you've done your work and understand what type of man you need, don't get distracted by going after something else. Stay on target and look for exactly what you want. Stick to your plan and go after what you have been looking for. Don't let anything stand in the way of that goal.

Make It Happen!

Going to the same places and meeting the same type of men will get you the same dating result. Break away from your patterns and try something new:

- Ignore your favorite hot spots and go somewhere else to have a fun evening out. Try different restaurants, dance clubs, or concert halls.

- Go to events sponsored by your professional organization, volunteer networks, or hobby groups.
- Visit your local museums, art festivals, and cultural events in your city.
- Go out with some new friends to one of their favorite hot spots.
- Borrow your friend's dog and take a walk at the dog park.
- Check out your local paper and go to an outdoor concert.

9

Go for It!

When new recruits come to boot camp, they're often overwhelmed when they hear what they'll be expected to accomplish. Many of them want to get right back on the bus! However, most determined men and women stay to be broken down and then rebuilt as stronger individuals. When they make it through the tough challenges and training drills—and get started on their real goals—their sense of pride and accomplishment is unstoppable.

You, too, have made it through the hardest part of your training and survived. The next challenge is to use your new skills and motivate yourself as you prepare to go back into the field.

You Made It Through Boot Camp!

Congratulations! You have completed your boot camp training! You should be very proud of yourself for doing all of the evaluation and refocusing necessary to be ready for the new dating environment. It's important to celebrate your accomplishment: go out and buy a new dress or a new pair of shoes. You're going to need some new things, because you're going to be using your new skills in the field very shortly.

In the meantime, it is important to realize a few things. First, remember to use your new training in all of your interactions with men, and leave your old habits behind. Change is challenging, but your new skills will eventually become natural to you.

Second, even though you may be excited to get out there, some of your friends may not be as enthusiastic about the new you. Don't be surprised if your changes are hard for them to accept. If the adjustment is rough for a while, remember that your changes are about you and no one else. Don't worry about what anyone else thinks.

Make It Happen!

You may be ready to launch a new initiative in the dating world, but people around you may not be as ready. Help your loved ones understand that the changes they see in you are nothing to worry about. Tell them ...

- You will try new dating methods, but you will be safe and use common sense in all situations.

- Many people date very successfully on the Internet, in dating services, and in singles clubs. You have to do new things to meet new people!

- There is nothing wrong with a woman approaching a man or asking a man out. Times have changed. Vehicles like the Internet, personal ads, and voice mail make it easy for women to take the lead.

142

- Your objective is a long-term relationship. While you're looking, your goal is to have fun and enjoy meeting interesting people.
- You're not necessarily trying to play the field. Instead, you're enjoying your single lifestyle until you meet the right one and commit.

Using Your New Skills

Tanya is shy and never really said much about her dating life. After going through boot camp, she learned how to solicit help in trying to get new dates. She told her friend Christina, who worked in a dentist's office, that she was looking to date someone new. Christina knew that the new hygienist, Mark, was single, so she facilitated a date for Tanya and Mark. A year later, they're still dating, thanks to Tanya stepping out of her comfort zone and sharing information about her dating desires.

You now have a variety of new tips and suggestions in your tool kit to help you improve your dating life. It's up to you to determine which ones work best for you. Try out what you've learned in different situations to find out which ones will help you get to the relationship that you want.

Like Tanya, it is your job to put these skills to use. Keep in mind that you might not like everything that you learn, and some things may be harder to master than others. This is your boot camp program, so shape it whatever way you need to. Get out and utilize what you have learned. Try every tip at least once so you can see what works for you. Step out of your comfort zone and embrace different things. Trying something new will help you get the results you are looking for.

You will never know what can happen if you don't try.

Make It Happen!

In boot camp, you have learned a number of new skills for your dating arsenal. Indicate by code which ones Work(W); which ones you need to Try (T); and which ones Don't work for you (D).

- ☐ Approached a man for small talk
- ☐ Approached a man for a date
- ☐ Dated more than one guy—plus one
- ☐ Dated more than one guy—plus two
- ☐ Dated more than one guy—plus three
- ☐ Dated more than one guy—four or more
- ☐ Signed up for a new class
- ☐ Committed to a new volunteer or hobby group
- ☐ Joined a singles group
- ☐ Tried online dating

☐ Participated in a singles mixer

☐ Went to a new nightclub

☐ Tried a new cultural event

☐ Changed appearance

☐ Improved attitude

☐ Bought new clothes/shoes

☐ Committed to going out three times monthly

☐ Committed to going out four times monthly

☐ Committed to going out five plus times monthly

☐ Reduced the number of commitments to other people

☐ Increased the number of dating commitments

☐ Left a key piece of personal baggage in the dust

☐ Used top-five assessment in meeting new men

After you have made your assessment, circle all of the items labeled with a T. Do you have a lot of these items? Then incorporate these items into your singles calendar and make plans to get out there and try some new things!

Leave the Past Behind

Michelle and Alberta had both completed Dating Boot Camp, and decided to go out and meet some new men at a local singles mixer. Both ladies looked outstanding and got a lot of attention. Michelle

*noticed the men looking and decided to take advan-
tage of it. She left the table and hung out near the
bar, looking friendly and approachable. A number of
men noticed and came up to chat. On the other hand,
Alberta didn't use any of her new skills and stayed at
the table. One guy did approach her, read her
nametag, and said, "Hello!" She shot him down
quickly, hoping someone better would come along.
Unfortunately, no one else did. Alberta left the mixer
feeling miserable—and very envious of Michelle.*

Now that you have a duffel bag of new skills, what happens to the old ones? Toss them to the wind! If what you
were doing didn't lead you to the relationship you want,
then leave it behind. Keep your focus on the things that
work for you and generate new results. Don't slip back
into your old way of doing things; it's easy to do because
it's what you know and is more comfortable. It's like being
on a diet. If you don't stick to your new eating habits,
you're going to get the same results. You don't want that
after the time and energy you put into your program.

It pays to get out there and just have a good time. The
more you do, the more you'll see that you have everything
you need to get what you want. Use your new skills and
techniques whenever you can; you already know what the
alternative will get you.

Make It Happen!

See how much your new techniques are helping you by doing a quick assessment. Compare what you were doing before with what you are doing now:

- Are you getting more dates than before?

- Do you feel better about yourself?

- Do you have the confidence to go for what you want?

- Are you excited about your single lifestyle?

- Do you have plans for the upcoming weekend?

- Is it easier to make plans when you want to now?

Use your new skills to their full advantage and keep enjoying yourself!

Preparing for the Opposition

When you're having this much fun, somebody's bound to try to burst your bubble. Unfortunately, not everyone is going to look at your dating success with full approval. Misery loves company, and when you decide to stop feeling bad about yourself, it may be easier for your miserable friends to attack you than to join you.

Don't be dismayed if some of your friends have negative reactions. There may be a reason for their negativity—they may not be ready for change themselves, or you just may be having more fun than they are. This may be especially true for your married friends. Let them live vicariously through you and try to understand them without letting them rain on your parade.

Dealing with Haters

> *Tammy took to her boot camp training like a duck to water. She pretty much had a date every weekend—she even found herself with the dilemma of dating two good men. One day, Tammy met a few of her girlfriends for lunch and couldn't wait to tell them all her great news. To her surprise, the reception was totally negative.*
>
> *"Do you really think you're going to get a relationship that way?"*
>
> *"I can't believe you're going out with two men."*
>
> *"I thought you wanted to get married!"*
>
> *Tammy couldn't believe the barrage of negative comments. These were her friends! Eventually, Tammy realized that her friends weren't able to understand her growth while they were still in a negative space. Instead of losing her cool, she bought them each a copy of* Dating Boot Camp *and wished them all good luck.*

You know from personal experience that, unfortunately, it's human nature to not always be as supportive as you can be of people that you care about. When someone you know is doing well, no matter how close you are, it's hard not to compare and feel bad if you're not doing as well.

It would be great if your friends and family members could jump up and down with pom-poms and tell you how great you're doing, but if they're not happy in their own lives, don't expect a miracle. Unhappy people are not always the best support group. If they're looking for dates and not getting any, or are stuck with somebody who doesn't make them happy, they may use you as a target.

Some of your friends may even think, "What is she doing to get all of the attention?" It's not that they don't want to see you happy, they're just not in their own happy place. Watch out for these unhappy people; they'll try to rain on your sunshine. Feel free to share your secrets—or give them this book as a gift. Either way, remember that everyone has the power to change their lives. You can't do it for them, so just worry about yourself and your own happiness.

Make It Happen!

Friends and family may mean to be supportive, but they sometimes don't know how to be. Here are some ways to deflect negative comments:

- If your mother tells you she doesn't like what you are doing, say, "I know you're concerned about me, but I'm making the best choices for me. I hope you can understand that."

continues

continued

- If your sister tells you that you'll only meet psychos on the Internet, say, "I didn't know you were Internet dating. How many psychos have you met?"

- If your girlfriend tells you that you are becoming too obsessed, say, "I have to give it my all; otherwise I will fail and not get what I want."

- If your ex tells you that he can't believe you're dating the way you are, tell him, "I decided to expand my dating possibilities. I have a clearer idea of what I want, and this time I'm going to get it."

Always tell your loved ones that you need support, not criticism. Tell them that the best way they can support you is to give you space to explore new opportunities, but be there if you need a shoulder to lean on.

Relying on Different Support Centers

Don't be mad at your friends if they don't understand the transition you have gone through. It takes a while for people to accept change, especially if they need to change themselves.

Try to surround yourself with people who are happy for you and the positive changes in your life. Friends who are supportive will realize that the changes are not just about getting some dates, but about enjoying your life. These friends may want to join you on some of your dating excursions or learn more about what you are doing. Use these friends as a sounding board for good and bad stories, to help you learn and grow in your dating lifestyle.

Relying on You
No matter what type of reception you get from your friends, you should always be your own best supporter. You've come a long way and should be proud of yourself. Having approval or acceptance from others feels good, but relying on yourself is more important. You made the changes in your life for *you*. Keep putting yourself first and you will find what you are seeking. Once you meet someone you can picture having a relationship with, you will be happy you did so much work up front. A good chunk of the hard work will be done, leaving more room for the good stuff: relationship building!

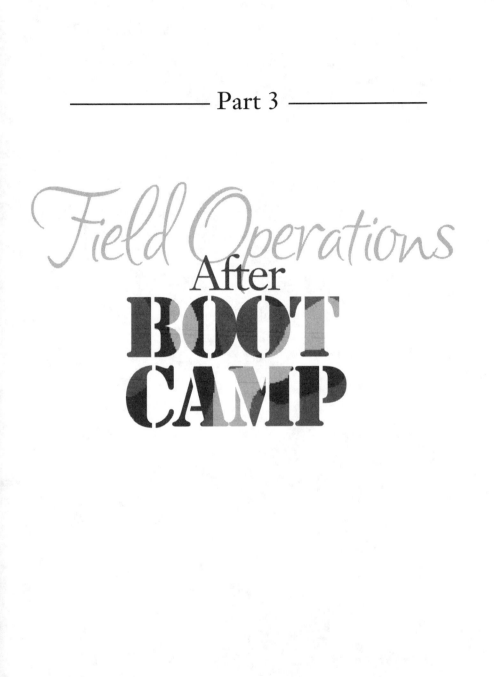

Part 3

Field Operations

After

BOOT
CAMP

10

Meeting and Interactions

You've made it through your boot camp training and now it's time for you to use your combat skills in the real world. Which of your new tools will work for you, and which ones won't be so easy to adapt? The only way to know is to get in the field and start meeting and interacting with men.

Don't worry, soldier—you're more than up to the task. You've got all the skills you need to make it work!

Completing the Last Part of Your Action Plan

The last part of your action plan helps you implement all of the skills you've learned through your training experience. This is your opportunity to explore new dating opportunities, empower yourself to make better dating choices, and stay in control. It's okay to make a man wait for a date, or even say "No"—it's up to you.

It's time to make a plan for what you want to achieve in your interactions. Work through the last part of your action plan to decide what you want and determine your steps to get there. This is your journey, no one else's. This plan doesn't have to fit what others think is appropriate: Make it work for *you*.

Implement

Implementing your plan is the final stage. This is your opportunity to put all of your training to work in the real world. Put on your gear and get ready!

In the following list, identify how you're going to implement your plan in each area. Shake things up and try things that push you out of your comfort zone.

1. Determine where to meet men:

   ♡ Gym   ♡ Grocery stores

   ♡ Work   ♡ Farmers markets

   ♡ Dance/jazz clubs   ♡ Art shows/exhibits

   ♡ Bars   ♡ Sports events

   ♡ Festivals   ♡ Community center

   ♡ Comedy clubs

2. Try new venues:

   ♡ Internet dating   ♡ Dating services

   ♡ Singles mixers   ♡ Networking groups

   ♡ Church   ♡ Activity clubs

   ♡ Speed dating   ♡ Singles parties

♡ Professional organizations ♡ Singles travel clubs

♡ Singles clubs ♡ Personal ads

♡ Singles adventure groups ♡ Volunteer organizations

♡ Parent groups

3. Start new actions:

   ♡ Say "Yes" to a dance

   ♡ Go out with someone who isn't your normal type

   ♡ Approach a guy and strike up a conversation

   ♡ Be receptive to a guy approaching you

   ♡ Invite a man out

   ♡ Go on a blind date

   ♡ Allow a friend to set you up

   ♡ Try a new hobby

4. Set new goals for this month:

   ♡ You will go out ___ number of times.

   ♡ You will meet ____ number of new men this month.

   ♡ You will go to ____ number of places to meet men.

   ♡ You will try ____ new venues to meet men this month.

Target Locations and Trying New Avenues

Your action plan options may look a little daunting, but you have to put yourself out there to meet new people. The man of your dreams is not going to show up at your door, and if you don't get out there, you'll never run into him.

Your dating lifestyle is about having fun, so pick things that you like to do. If you enjoy yourself, others will see that and want to be around you. If you can't see yourself at the gym, then that's not the place for you to meet men. If you're open to the gym, but you've never attended a class, get out of your comfort zone and sign up for a spinning class. No one's pushing you to do something completely out of character; however, you have to do something different to get a different result.

Drill Sergeant Says ...

Remember that you're not just branching out to meet people, you're enhancing your single lifestyle. Do things that you find fun and interesting, and you'll meet people who are just as excited as you are to try new activities. You'll feel great just having a good time.

Same Place, Different Venue

What if you've already tried some of the places listed to meet men before? A club is a club is a club, right? Not necessarily. If going to a club always means the same one or the same type, then yes, you'll probably see the same people. Expand your boundaries and mix up where you go. Try a club in a different part of town—or a different town altogether. By surveying different locales, you will meet more single people. These singles may have friends or a network that you haven't even tapped into. Get out of the bunker and explore! You'll be surprised at what you find.

Make It Happen!

Try to mix it up by meeting people in the same kinds of places, but at different locations:

- Clubs—try different ones: salsa, hip-hop, jazz lounge, dance clubs, or reggae.

- Gym—try a different routine: sign up for a different class or special training, or attend special events that your gym may offer, such as a health fair or promotional event.

- Festivals—there are all kinds of festivals you can attend: wine tasting, music in the park, Shakespeare, art, harvest, boating, dedications, and other cultural events.

- Grocery store—everybody has to go shopping, so why don't you go to different stores around you: go to a different grocery store in your neighborhood or check out the higher-end food market or even the specialty food stores. Many grocery stores or markets have a deli and sit-down area where you can have lunch and meet people.

- Farmers' market—most cities have a farmers' market: check out a different one every time you go.

continues

continued

- Community center—you probably haven't checked out your local community center: take a class, learn a new hobby, or just meet other people in your neighborhood.

- Dinner parties—attend a friend's dinner party or have one of your own: if you host, you can require that each guest brings a new friend. If you go to one, go solo to give yourself room to mix and mingle.

- Get-togethers—these events can take on a life of their own when the host has a theme or provides get-together games. Get-togethers are a great way to get off the couch and interact with people in a relaxed and fun environment.

- Friend network—you'd be surprised whom your friends know, and there may be some gems waiting to be hooked up with you. Don't underestimate the power of a great referral from a friend. You can get information about your date before you meet him, and your friends already know you, so they know what you're looking for!

- Wine tastings—brush up your wine knowledge *and* meet new people. You can mix and mingle with other wine connoisseurs while you drink wine, listen to music, or learn about the winery.

- Church—expanding your network at your place of worship is a great way to meet people with similar spiritual beliefs. You can attend socials, singles Bible study, and other church activities that will help you interact with people right in your own world.

- Book clubs—if you are an avid reader, join a book club. There are clubs that are specific to a certain book genre or ones that cater to different types of readers, such as singles or a certain age group.

New Venues, New Opportunities

You have a lot of new experiences to conquer as a single woman. Many women are unaware of all the different dating channels they have at their fingertips. Don't feel like you're doing things just because you're desperate to meet a man. A lot of singles events are fun ways to meet new people and do something enjoyable at the same time. When you are in the mindset of being open to new experiences, you will meet new people and possibly the guy you have been looking for. So, get in the field and try new things! See Appendix A for more resources.

Make It Happen!

There are a lot of fun things to do if you are open to exploring. Be adventurous and step into something new:

- Internet dating. Everyone is either meeting people online or thinking about it. Choose from a variety of sites, and either post your profile or just respond to others. Internet dating is an easy way to reach people who are looking for a relationship, but have a tough

continues

continued

time finding time to mingle. Take your time screening
the men you meet and use your common sense in determining whether or not you should meet them. For more
Internet dating tips, see Appendix A.

- Singles mixers. Mixers are a great way to meet new
  people and do something fun at the same time. If you're
  not sure about Internet dating, some dating sites like
  Match.com have a calendar of singles activities. Attend
  events such as movie nights, comedy nights, cooking
  classes, or a job-networking function. Events are either
  set up by age group or are open for all adults.

- Singles clubs. The clubs have helped a number of
  women meet men. The types of clubs can vary, but they
  typically are comprised of people who want to meet more
  interesting people. Some of these clubs focus on activities such as dancing, community service, travel, music,
  reading, dining, cultural events, and sports outings.

- Singles adventure groups. These are for singles who
  like to indulge in more rigorous sports. These groups
  have activities such as hiking, kayaking, camping, water
  sports, skiing, and even extreme sports. Most people
  are in these groups because they love what they are
  doing, while others are new and want to learn the ropes.

- Speed dating. This new trend condenses the time it
  takes to meet people so that you can meet more people. You meet people, have a few minutes to chat, and
  follow up with people you like through their websites.

Some groups have a mixer activity such as a dance lesson or some type of show. Speed dating is quick and fun and keeps you on your toes.

- Professional organizations. There are professional groups to help you groom your public-speaking abilities, manage your finances, network for jobs, enhance your career, mentor business youth, and so on. Take some time to pick a group that will help you professionally and expose you to other people in your career field.

- Community service groups. In any city, there are always a number of community service groups that could spark your interest, from helping the disabled to sponsoring park clean-up days. Look in your local paper for groups asking for volunteers. You'll work side by side with people who care about your common interests and get a chance to hang out afterward with them.

- Arts organizations. Go see a community theater performance or attend museum openings. Most art, music, or theatrical groups have a membership group, and you will be invited to a number of cultural events that suit your interest.

- Political groups. If you have a strong interest in politics, join a campaign or canvas for a cause. You'll meet new people who have similar interests in political topics, and you can participate in change within your country.

163

Interacting with a Guy

Now that you see through the camouflage and know where to meet them, how do you interact with them? Be confident, and know that if a man is attracted to you, everything else should fall into place. Have a conversation with him and keep him interested in getting to know you better. The key is to keep your confidence level up and know that he is interacting with you because you're just being yourself. Don't freak out and get all fumbled up. Simply talk with him as you would with anybody and let the conversation flow.

When a Guy Approaches—What to Do?

Depending on the setting, if a man approaches you to chat, you should feel comfortable doing just that. If you're at a casual event, he may come up to you and ask you how you're doing and maybe offer you a drink. If it is a more formal affair, he may not be as direct. He may ask who you know at the event, then ask if you would like a beverage.

Either way, he's just trying to find a way to break the ice and start a conversation. Your goal is to interact with him so you can be in control of the situation. Chat with him enough to subtly let him know you are interested; if you're not, you can easily put on your camouflage and duck out of the conversation without being offensive.

Make It Happen!

If you are interested:

- Be friendly and inviting by smiling and nodding when he is speaking.

- Tell him about yourself and be open to his questions.

- Ask him questions about himself and look for similar interests the two of you may have.

- Give him a lead-in to ask you out. For instance, if you know that both of you like jazz, tell him that you noticed that your favorite jazz pianist is performing at a local venue. If he's interested in asking you out, he'll pick up on the opportunity.

- If he asks for your phone number, give him your cell phone number and a good time for him to reach you.

If you're not interested:

- Keep your interaction as brief as possible.

- Be friendly and engage in conversation, but keep your answers short.

- Stage and deploy an exit if necessary. If you really don't want to speak to him any longer, tell him that your friends are looking for you across the way and you need to go over to them.

continues

continued

- If he asks you out, tell him you are seeing someone currently and make your way out of the conversation.
- Politely exit by telling him that it was nice speaking to him.

It's Okay to Approach a Guy

In some instances you may see someone you want to meet. Is it okay to make the first move? If you haven't gathered by now, the answer is "Yes!"

Nowadays, men are more comfortable with women making the first move. The key is to not feel intimidated about approaching someone. If you look like a deer caught in headlights, he will pick up on it and wonder why you're even speaking to him. On the other hand, if you approach confidently, he'll be more intrigued and want to speak to you. Before you approach, have some kind of plan in place so you have something to say when you're standing in front of him.

If he is receptive, be ready with more conversation points to throw his way. If he's not, have your exit plan in place so you won't look like he shot you down.

Make It Happen!

Before you approach him, know what you're going to say:

- Use your environment to leverage a conversation. For example, if he's standing alone at an art exhibit , walk up to him and ask him what he thinks the artist is saying with the piece.

- If you know someone at the event, have her introduce you. Tell your friend that you want to meet him, have her make the introductions, and then arrange for her to leave the two of you to talk.

- Let him know you have something in common. If he's tapping his foot to a song, tell him you really like it, too. Use this as a chance to talk about music.

Notice how receptive he is to you. If he's interested:

- Ask him how he's enjoying the event and share how much you are enjoying it as well.

- Ask him more questions about himself: his job, his interests, his dating status ....

- Let him know you're interested by telling him it was nice meeting him and you hope to see him again. If he's interested, he'll probably ask for your phone number or at least offer his.

continues

continued

If he doesn't seem interested:

- Make it clear that you were just being friendly and exit the conversation by saying "Hey, have a great evening!"
- Mention something about a boyfriend to imply that you weren't trying to pick him up.
- Let him know you're just having a good time meeting people—that way he won't think you were targeting him as a potential date.

Keep the Interaction Positive

If you find yourself in a conversation, keep it positive. Even if you're interested in going out with him, remember to not rush things, and keep the conversation light. A man can pick up on nervousness, anxiety, and impatience, so let things flow naturally. Relax and enjoy yourself, and show that you are enjoying the conversation. Talk about things that interest you both and don't let the conversation get too heavy. Stay away from talking about anything that would be better suited for future dates, such as the following subjects:

♡ Things you like about sex

♡ The guilt your mother places on you

♡ Emotional issues you are trying to overcome

♡ Bad relationship tales

♡ Really bad relationship tales

♡ Things he likes about sex

♡ His ex or your ex

♡ Any other relationship-oriented topic you should reserve for when you are in a relationship.

The best way to keep the interaction positive is to have self-confidence. The better you feel about yourself, the more you will shine. You have all the tools you need, and the only way to win is to stay in the game. So charge ahead and win!

11

The First Date

A first date can be magical or it can be a total disaster. It's when you really start getting to know someone, and, as most girls know, there might be fireworks or it might be an endurance test.

Face it, first dates can be downright scary. You have to get him interested in you, and keep him interested in you. You have to say the right things and act the right way, and even after all of that, he still may not call.

Acing the Interview

You may be thinking, "Why does it have to be that hard?" Well, it doesn't. A lot of women put more energy into the first date than they need to. If you look at a first date for what it is, it can take some of the pressure off. It's simply a brief meeting with someone you might like to get to know better—period.

Think of your first date as being similar to a job interview. You meet with the interviewer to help him or her get to know you while you learn more about the company and the opportunity. You present yourself in the best light and, if all goes well, you'll have a second interview.

A first date is basically the same thing; both parties have to feel interested and comfortable with one another. Some experts say men are able to decide within the first 15 minutes whether or not they want to go on another date. Women, on the other hand, take a little longer. Women will give men more of a chance and wait to see where the date is headed before they draw a conclusion.

Take the opportunity to let him really get a good assessment of you. Help him see the funny, classy, sexy, spunky, smart woman you are. You won't get a second chance, so grab this moment. If you got to the date, there was obviously something that sparked his interest. Put a flame under that interest and showcase the things he likes about you. More than likely, he'll want to see more of you.

Even if you don't get a second date out of it, there are many more men out there who are interested in who you are. Women often put more effort into being the perfect person than paying attention to what kind of impression the guy is making. They also often forget to have fun! Try this: When you're on your next first date, make the most of it. Enjoy whatever you are doing, *then* decide if you want to have another date with this person.

Common Mistakes Women Typically Make

Now that you're on the date you've been hoping for all these months, you wouldn't do anything to mess it up, right? Unfortunately, you may have no idea you did anything wrong—until you find yourself wondering why he hasn't called. Did you miss something? It can't be you, can it? In your mind, the date went well, but what is *he* thinking? Who knows?

The following sections provide tips on what not to do on the first date. If you haven't been on a first date in a long time, you might need to brush up on the peculiarities of the male mind and be aware of some things to avoid. Don't find yourself wondering, "What did I do wrong?"

Wanting Too Much Too Soon

> *Sherrie had finally met someone she "clicked" with. She'd been waiting for this man forever! Even though it was her first date with Ivan, she just knew they were going to be together. They had already interacted well at Susie's party, and all her friends told her that they'd make a great couple. She already had a list of things they could do together. All they had to do was have dinner, and soon they'd be planning weekend activities for months to come ....*

Sherrie had it all planned. The only thing missing was the man to agree to it! Women are great when it comes to making arrangements, seating charts, and forecasts of the future. Sometimes it's appropriate; other times, it's complete self-sabotage.

A lot of women who have great friends, successful careers, and financial stability are usually missing one thing—the man. But you can't just expect to find the perfect man to perfectly fit into your established life. This man has to be a real fit, not something to check off your list. If you meet a nice man, the fact that he seems nice is *all you know about him* until you spend more time with him. Go out with him—more than once—before you decide he's someone whom you want to stick around. Take time to get to know him before you invite him to your next five social events.

Even if he's a good fit, when he sees you coming at him with your Day Planner, he will surely run the other way. Men can be terrified of commitment, especially when you're making long-term plans and they're not even sure how much they like you. Pressuring him for other activities before you finish the first course at dinner will more than likely squash your chances at Date #2.

Make It Happen!

Take pressure off of your first date by keeping the interaction light and staying in the moment.

Don't ...

- Allude to anything in the future that relates to you as a couple.
- Make suggestions of where you can go for the next five dates.

- Assume you'll have another date before it's time to discuss it—preferably at the end of the date.

- Get too close too quickly by asking him when you are going to meet his friends or family.

- Forget that he doesn't really know you or your personality. Steer clear of jokes or comments that could be offensive, or just weird.

- Tell him your entire life history in one sitting. Let the conversation flow—don't dominate, but don't be afraid to talk, either!

Do ...

- Relax and have a good time.

- Follow his lead if he suggests getting together again (that is, if *you* want to go out with him again).

- Remember that he's a date, not your boyfriend. Keep the touching and overt flirting to a minimum.

- Take your dates one at a time.

- Get to know your date well before you invite him to your next social occasion.

- Leave the Day Planner at home.

- Let him know what you like to do without strongly suggesting he do it with you.

Making Him "The One"

Don't feel bad: Every woman at one time or another has done it. She meets a guy who seems perfect for her. The next thing you know she starts putting her first name with his last name and fantasizing about the wedding day, what her dress will look like, and how the kids will look. All of this can sometimes happen even before the first date!

A lot of women are looking for the perfect relationship. A lot of women want to get married. There's nothing wrong with these notions. The problem comes when every positive interaction with a man becomes a prelude to the perfect wedding. Too much fantasizing can be destructive when you don't even know the guy. Spend your time learning more about him, learning what made you think this in the first place. Stay objective so you can determine your real feelings about him.

True, nice men do exist. However, not every one you meet is going to be "The One." The right guy will have a number of things that make you want to be with him. Note what moves you. The right guy will have most of these qualities and you'll know right away if he could be "The One"—if you really know what you're looking for.

Make It Happen!

Make your interaction with your date more about what you *want* to know about him than what you *think* you know about him.

Don't ...

- Continue to make every man you meet your future husband.
- Get so caught up in projecting the future that you miss getting to know your date.
- Overlook how the two of you are interacting.
- Put too much pressure on your date to act in the perfect way you want him to. Allow him to feel comfortable enough to be himself.

Do ...

- Become more aware of what makes you think a man is "The One." Is it because he has a great quality, or is it simply because he paid attention to you? Really determine what is driving you into this mental rush down the aisle.
- Note what you really want from a future mate and use this to learn more about you, not to make your date into something he's not.
- Slow down and enjoy your date.
- Take time to learn what great qualities your date has.
- Let him get to know you as much as you need to know him.

Don't Be Needy!

All women want to feel cared for and attended to. However, when a man perceives this as being whiny, wimpy, or helpless, you're in trouble.

> *Mike was really looking forward to his date with Sandra. She was attractive, a real go-getter, and seemed to know what she wanted. However, from the time he picked her up to the time he dropped her off, she seemed like a different person. Sandra didn't have her own opinion about anything, she wouldn't let him out of her sight, and she was hanging on him all night. She didn't seem like the woman he met at the networking luncheon. Mike drove away knowing he wouldn't be asking Sandra out again.*

It's nice to have a man in your life. He is someone you can do things with, hang out with, and just *be* with. It's hard if you really want this kind of relationship and you don't have it.

However, *you don't have to let the guy you're with know how much you miss it!* Being too needy is like a repellent for most men. Your date reads that as meaning you'll hang on him, being whiny and fussy all the time. Basically, it's a major turnoff.

Drill Sergeant Says ...

Be yourself on your date, but don't show every emotion you have in one night. Even if you feel lonely, you don't have to show your date you're feeling that way.

Instead of showing him how much you miss having a man, show him what kind of woman you are. Everyone gets lonely—he may be lonely, too. But you don't want to show him a side of you that is not representative of who you really are and the person he wants to get to know.

Make It Happen!

Don't let neediness ruin your date. Instead, be confident and let him really get to know you.

Don't ...

- Hang all over him on the first date.
- Look like you are hawking his every move if he goes to the bar or to the bathroom.
- Be whiny, cutesy, or just plain irritating.
- Talk about being lonely, wanting a man in your life, or anything else to give the impression that he's not going to be able to wrench you from his side.

continues

continued

Do ...

- Realize that being a damsel in distress is not the way to get a man.
- Use what you have to get what you want, but use only the positive things, like your personality and ambition.
- Give yourself a chance to shine without being needy.
- Act like your normal self.
- Present yourself in a self-assured manner and expect him to relate to you as such.
- Be direct about what you want without sounding like you have been waiting for him to come into your life.
- Keep your conversation and your interaction light.

Don't Be Too Eager!

Tina hadn't been on a good date in months. She was going out with Brad and she couldn't wait to show him how happy she was. She was peppy and enthusiastic about everything he had to say. Whenever he suggested going somewhere, Tina was super-excited. She thought her enthusiasm would show Brad that she was the right girl for him. Instead, Brad thought she was a little weird.

Being excited about meeting someone is normal. Being *too* excited can be construed as weird. Keep in mind, guys do have a hard time finding the kind of women that they would like to date long-term. Men rarely find it hard to just get a date, so they cannot relate to your enthusiasm at *finally* meeting someone nice, someone with whom you have things in common, and, most importantly, someone who just seems *normal*.

Even if this is the case, keep your excitement under control. Every time he mentions his parents or his friends, don't say how great it would be to meet them, even if he suggests it. You can be excited, but you don't want him to think he's the first man who's taken you out in a long time—even if he is. Be cool. Take it for what it is, relax, and enjoy.

Make It Happen!

It's okay to be excited about your date, but when you are on the date, focus on getting to know each other. You may find that there may be much more to be excited about!

Don't ...

- Act like this date is the only one you will ever have.
- Use your date as a therapy session to talk about your ex, your children's father, or other relationships.
- Let your excitement make the date itself more important than the man you are trying to get to know.

continues

continued

Do ...

- Enjoy your date for the experience—have fun and appreciate the company without going overboard.

- Feel good! It's okay to be excited—just don't take it over the top.

- Put your positive energy into getting to know your date better and letting him learn things about you.

- Remember, the date is more than the activity—what you are doing can be fun, but the objective is to get to know the other person, too.

Apply Your New Techniques

When you see the objectives of your first date clearly, you can see that it's not just about what you're doing, it's about what you want to get out of it. If your goal is to just hang out and have a good time, then do just that. If your goal is to enjoy yourself, but learn key things about your date, then do that as well.

You have the ability to move your date in the direction you want it to go and get exactly what you want out of it. The following sections explain how to set yourself up for success.

Be Your Charming Self

It may sound like an old cliché, but men really expect and want you to be yourself. Ask men what is one of the most irritating things on a date and they all say they *hate* it when a woman is not herself.

Be yourself—that's who he asked out! He engaged in enough contact or conversation with you and wanted to get to know you better. He obviously liked what he saw and what you had to say in order to get this far. Don't forget that!

Realizing this should take off some of that first-date pressure. He's doesn't want you to be anyone other than yourself. In addition, you don't have to look better than you ever have in your life to go on this date. Just be yourself.

Exude Confidence

Feel good about this man who wants to go out with you. He recognizes how great you are and wants to get to know more about you. This is your opportunity to learn more about him and see if he is worthy of your attention. It is okay to show your confidence. The key is to exhibit this confidence without being smug or cocky. Men are attracted to assertiveness, but they tend to find cockiness in a woman a big turnoff.

Have a strong presence, feel confident in your demeanor and your interaction, and be decisive. If he asks you where you want to go after dinner and you want to go out for coffee, don't say, "Oh, I don't know—what do you want to do?" He asked you, didn't he? Instead, tell him, "I would love to go out for coffee. My favorite spot is around the corner."

He will appreciate you telling him what you want to do and not being wishy-washy about it. Also, by being nice about how you tell him what you want, he will feel good and not feel like you're trying to tell him what to do. Your level of confidence will make him feel more at ease if he is nervous or unsure of himself.

Be in Control Without Appearing Controlling

Men like women who are in control, but have a problem with women who seem like they are trying to control them. It is a fine tightrope to walk. The best way to do this is to know what you want for yourself and suggest what you would like for him. Men hate for women to tell them what to do, but love it when women can be supportive of the ideas they come up with themselves.

For instance, if you would like white wine with your entrée and he's determined to order the wine for both of you, casually mention that you love white wine and it would be great if they had a particular brand. He will take the lead and see if the restaurant has your brand. If they don't, he'll be inclined to get another white wine that *he* suggests. Throw in a comment like, "I'm sure any white wine you select would be great."

Remember, this man is trying to impress you, so let him. A little guidance won't stop him, but will ensure that you get what you want, too. You can get what you want from men without being bossy. Be suggestive without being pushy.

Manage the Conversation

In conversation on a first date, you walk a fine line of telling the man enough information about you without giving away the farm. On the other hand, he wants to tell you about himself, but doesn't want to say the wrong thing and run you off.

Let him learn just enough about you, and try to learn just what you need to know about him. It's not hard to achieve this; you just have to know what to say and what to avoid. Tell him about …

- ♡ Your interests.
- ♡ Your career aspirations.
- ♡ Your current occupation.
- ♡ Your hobbies.
- ♡ Your everyday life.
- ♡ Your family.
- ♡ Your pet (just don't sound like a cat lady).

Avoid telling him about …

♡ Your ex.

♡ Why your relationships fail.

♡ Extreme family dramas.

♡ Your pet peeves.

♡ Your fears.

♡ Things that make you depressed.

♡ Sexual preferences—or sexual issues.

♡ Serious health issues.

♡ Financial problems.

♡ Problems with your girlfriends.

♡ Things that make you seem really opinionated.

And it goes without saying that it's best to avoid common hot topics such as politics and religion. Save those for later in the relationship if you can.

The best advice in managing the conversation is to keep it light. Avoid saying anything that *you* wouldn't want to hear. Direct your questions towards learning more about him. Get information that you feel is important to know in determining whether you'd like to go out with him again.

Conversation is an information exchange, not full disclosure. Keep things relevant but easy-going. Future dates with him will help determine whether or not he is the person with whom you will share your deep dark secrets. In the meantime, keep them to yourself.

Avoid Those Conversation Pitfalls

Great conversation is the key to a successful first date. Keep the topics general, fun, and engaging. You're getting to know one another, and talking about things you're both interested in will help you achieve this. Think about the interview analogy—you want to learn more about him just as he wants to learn more about you. However, you don't want to divulge too much about yourself before he really knows you. Here are some suggestions to help you avoid stalling your interaction:

Oversharing

There's a fine line between sharing aspects and interests of your life and delving too deeply into territory best left for later. Learn the difference between oversharing and sharing just enough to spark a common interest. Try just bringing a topic up in passing, then letting it go. If he's interested, he'll pursue it.

For example, if you're a regular churchgoer, that's certainly something important to share. But it's possible to drop that information in passing without dwelling on it so much that you come off as someone with no life outside of church. The same rules apply to your hobbies and your job. If he feels like your life is already too full, he'll wonder if there's room for him in it.

Taboo Topics

You may feel it's important to know his financial status, his religious background, and how he's going to vote in the presidential election, but you have to be careful bringing up these topics. If you continue to have a relationship with this guy, you'll learn more about him every time you interact with him. Don't be in such a rush! Conversations about financial status, religion, politics, and sex can be pretty explosive if you strike a chord of disagreement.

Keep the conversation on lighter, "getting-to-know-you" topics, and broach the more controversial conversations later in your relationship.

The Know-It-All Syndrome

You want your date to like you for who you are. If you're smart, he probably already likes that about you, so you don't have to showcase it. Your date probably doesn't want to talk about brain-intensive issues, he just wants to enjoy your company and have a good time. So don't overdo it. Men like smart women, but they don't want to feel like they're taking a Mensa exam.

If you're smart, you shouldn't have to prove it in your conversation. You don't have to play dumb, but you may need to relax and interact with him on a more conversational level. It's not bad to say, "Hey, did you read that article about astrophysics in the *Wall Street Journal* this morning?" On the other hand, it would probably be a turnoff to go into great analytical detail about why the reporter's research was all wrong. Men think smart is sexy, but being too smart can be intimidating and a turnoff.

Also, controversial or emotional topics that lead to heated debates are *not* the way to go. Your goal is to enjoy your date, not make it challenging or unbearable. Keep it light and you will have more things to talk about on your next date!

Make Him Want More of You

On your date, you want to be yourself, say what you need to for your date to know you better, and keep him interested in you. He is learning about you and you are learning what you need to know about him. Hopefully, you're also having fun and getting more curious about each other.

How can you ensure that you can get him intrigued about you? The main thing to do is show that you are interested in him. A lot of times, women expect men to be mind-readers. Men are really poor at this. Instead, show and tell him what you want.

Show Interest in Him

Every woman knows that the male ego is alive and kicking. Men want to know that the woman they are interested in finds them just as interesting. On your date, give the male ego the attention it needs. The way to pinpoint what he finds important is to observe what he talks about the most. If he talks about his job a lot, then obviously his job is really important to him. Ask questions to show that you're curious about it, too. Listen to what he has to say, nodding and showing acknowledgement. By showing interest in him, you'll make him feel important. Every guy is more interested in someone who's interested in him! Show your interest in him throughout the date, and he will reciprocate his level of interest in you.

It's All About You, Too

The flip side to being interested in him is to ensure that you're not becoming president of his fan club. You can show your interest and stroke his ego, but you don't want to act like everything is about him. He should be just as interested in you, asking you questions about yourself and showing that he is interested in what you have to say.

It's easy to get involved in learning things about him and not notice that he isn't really showing an interest in you. There has to be a balance. If you have to double-check to ensure that he's showing as much interest in you as you are in him, here are some questions to ask yourself:

♡ Does he talk without asking you much about you?

♡ Does he acknowledge that he has been one-sided in his interaction?

♡ What kinds of things does he want to know about you?

♡ Do his questions make you feel like he wants to know more about you?

♡ Are you feeling bored with what he has to say?

If you realize that he's mostly consumed with himself, you *can* do something about it. A lot of women will just let the man drone on about himself. Take charge and let him know what he's doing. Interject a question like: "So, Bob, I'm learning a lot about you—what do you want to know about me?"

This should help him acknowledge that he's tried to make the date all about him. Shake him up a bit and let him know that it's not! Give him a chance to correct himself and turn the topic back to you. If he doesn't get the clue, you have to decide how much more of a one-sided date you're in the mood for. If you've had enough, you can feel okay about ending it. If he doesn't want to lose you, he'll snap to attention and give you the attention that you need.

Be Flirty

What man can resist a woman who is flirting with him? If you're attracted to your date, it's okay to let him know it. Communicate that you are interested by simply showing him. It's not what you say, it's how you say it.

Every woman has a signature flirty thing she does to keep a man intrigued. It could be how you throw your hair or how you say his name. Give him signals to let him know that you're interested in him. Sit closer to him, look him directly in the eye, smile as you talk, laugh lightly at his funny comments. Men love it when women openly flirt with them because it lets them gauge their level of interest.

If you're interested, make sure he gets the message. Keep in mind that being flirty doesn't take away from how intelligent or serious you are. It's just a way to be more open in conveying your interest. Let your hair down and feel free to be flirty!

Leave a Little Intrigue

As you get to know this man, don't tell him things you wouldn't tell anyone else who doesn't know you that well. In addition, leave a little mystery about yourself and give him something to find out about you. Women intrigue men by the way they think and the things that they do. Men love the mystery of a woman.

Keep him wondering. On your date, don't tell him your entire life story. If you tell him things about yourself, don't disclose all the details. If he wants to continue to get to know you, then little chunks of information are good enough to get you started. A good way to keep yourself from disclosing too much is to tell him what he wants to know, then ask him a question about himself.

For instance, if he asks you about what you do, tell him exactly that: "I am a veterinarian." If he asks you why you became one, again, succinctly answer: "I've just always loved animals. I couldn't see myself doing anything else!" Then ask him about his career. "So, what made you so fascinated with computer programming?" By being concise with your answers, you avoid telling him too many details and have a more equal exchange. But be careful not to cut off your answers *too* quickly. Remember, the conversation needs to be easygoing and natural.

Things to Get Him to Ask You Out Again

So, you had a great date. You both seemed to enjoy each other's company and you think he's going to ask you out again. But how can you be sure?

There's no magic formula, but you *can* make it easier. Men can get intimidated even when things are going well, and sometimes they don't know how to take the next step. Do your part by interacting with him positively, and taking some of the pressure off.

Leave an Open Pathway

You had a good time, but how can you be sure he knows that? Women expect men to pick up on the obvious. Sometimes they can, and sometimes they ask anyway, but sometimes they just drop the ball.

You want him to know you're on the same page. Smile and let him know you had a good time and you'd like to see him again. You don't have to ask him out, exactly, but you can let him know that you want him to ask you out. If sometime during your evening he mentioned anything that he thought it would be fun for you to do together, bring it up again. Tell him, " If you ever want to have that dart competition, I'm up for it!"

You've not only let him know that the date was good, you've also given him an idea for the next date—and an "in" to do the asking. If he was hoping to ask you out again, but didn't know how to get around to it, you just made it easy for him. More than likely, he will!

Let It Fit, Don't Force It

It's fine to give a man the green light, but you have to let him put his own foot on the gas. Too many women let a guy know how they are feeling, then go too far by trying to push him. He may need you to let him know that you want to see him again, but it should be a comfortable exchange, so that either one of you can ask about the next date without it feeling weird. If you're too pushy, you may not get the results you are looking for. He might feel too obligated and want to run!

It sounds crazy, but too many guys have said this is the case. Allow him to set up the date, and if he doesn't, then leave it to him. Either he's not ready, or he needs time to pull himself together. Give him the opportunity to show his interest. Maybe he didn't have the courage to step up in person, but will give you a call to follow through. This may sound silly to a woman who knows what she wants, but face it, sometimes men need a little extra room to step it up.

When You Have Other Things to Do

Even though you're itching for this man to ask you out, don't be too available. If he asks you out during the date, don't immediately say "Yes." Give him a tentative "Yes," then tell him that you'll give him a call to confirm. You don't want him thinking you've got nothing to do but to wait on him!

Instead, you want him to be wondering whether you can fit him into your schedule. Never give the impression that you're sitting at home waiting for him to call.

By keeping yourself busy, you won't be so consumed with wondering whether he's going to call you, should you call him, and all of that. If he didn't ask you out and said he would call you, make other plans. If he calls and you've already made plans for Saturday, don't break them! Make plans with him for Sunday—and you *don't* have to tell him what you're doing Saturday.

Your single lifestyle is about *you*, until you find exactly what you're looking for. A potential second date isn't enough for you to decide that this man is "The One." Keep dating and doing other things until you're sure. Remember: A woman with a busy schedule is *not* waiting on a man.

When You Don't Get the Call

What happens if you had a great date and he doesn't call? Don't worry about it! You don't know why he didn't call, so don't blame yourself. Don't bother wondering why he

195

didn't call. If he didn't, he's obviously not serious about wanting to get to know you and isn't worth any more of your time.

Chalk it up to you had a great date and move on. Not every date will end in a love connection. It's more important to have fun and keep putting yourself out there.

12

Your Second Date and Beyond— Relationship Stages

You made it through the obstacle course, survived the drills, had a great first date, and are finally dating someone with whom you think you could have a relationship. Before you let yourself flip head over heels, make sure you're in the right frame of mind for a relationship and understand the rules for having one.

A common mistake women make is focusing more on the fact that they have a relationship than on the person they're with. Don't get so caught up in trying to have the perfect relationship that you don't enjoy it when things are good—or miss the signs when things are not so good.

It's easy to focus on the date planning, gift giving, and "couple" events, especially when you haven't had a steady guy for a while. But putting too much of your focus there can not only stress you out, it can stress your guy out enough that he might think he'd be better off not being in a relationship. Men do enjoy the security and affection of a relationship with a special woman, but when things get too orchestrated, they sometimes go AWOL.

You don't want this to be the reason your relationship fails. There's nothing wrong with wanting more from your relationship; let it happen naturally. Enjoy being in the moment with him and let the relationship progress. By taking more time to discover your role in the relationship, you'll be more analytical about your interactions with your partner, and recognize when you need to take a closer look at yourself.

Relationship Reality

You worked really hard to find the kind of relationship you want, but now is when the *real* work begins. Going out for fabulous evenings, learning new stories about each other, and feeling good about your potential together—that's called "dating." Relationships are about more than that.

A relationship is about two people agreeing to be together, and dealing with one another during the good times and the bad. Women seek relationships to escape from the lonely times, then realize they can still have lonely times if they're in the wrong relationship.

The key is to understand right off the bat that men have different perceptions of the stages of a relationship than women do. When you see it from both sides, you can find common ground and make your relationship workable and happy.

What Women See

If you ask a woman what she wants most out of life, she will usually say a wonderful man, a great career, and a family—with the wonderful man at the top of the list.

Along with the great man is the fantasy wedding. Women dream of the day that they'll say "I do"—the gown, the cake, the location, and the honeymoon. Women grow up dreaming of this perfect vision and want to live out the fantasy. The finale is having a family with this great man and living happily ever after.

A woman tends to view a relationship as integral to her success in the world. Her goal is to have the best relationship and grow closer and closer to her man; the closer the better. She'll even shut out her girlfriends and be totally engrossed in her relationship, hoping to drive it to the next level. Her goal is to seal the deal so the next phase of her life can begin.

What Men See

This may shock you, but men don't see things the same way. Men aren't typically raised to place the same primary focus on marriage or long-term companionship. This doesn't mean they don't want the same thing—it just means the road they take to get there may be a little different.

Some men see a relationship as a loss of freedom. Some even go so far as to say that being in a relationship is a permanent loss of their individualism. On the other hand, there are men who really want to be married, but need to really be ready so they don't make the wrong decision. Let's explore how different types of guys approach this topic.

The Not-So-Sure Guy

This is the guy who wants to have a long-term commitment and even marriage with a woman he loves, but he really needs to be sure he's making the right choice. He may have dated a few women, but he usually evaluates them for wife potential from the first meeting. He's sincere, but paranoid, and can become so fearful that he doesn't do anything to move the relationship along; he just keeps waiting for that sign to tell him he's sure.

If you are dating a Not-So-Sure Guy, show him the value of your relationship and that you two are a good match. The more easygoing you are, the better. Don't put too much pressure on him, just nudge him in the right direction. Tell him how happy you are being together and reassure him that your relationship is a good one. Eventually, he'll see that there's nothing to be afraid of and be more open to a long-term commitment.

Peter Pan

This type of man is all about hanging out and having fun. His whole objective is to enjoy life and not stress out about things. He's fun to go out with and can keep you entertained for hours. He enjoys having you as a companion, but a lot of times he can't see anything beyond that. He isn't big on responsibility, but he continues to date you, even exclusively.

The challenge comes when you want more. Peter Pan likes to hang out with Wendy, but he doesn't want her dictating what time he needs to come home. He wants to be free, and having a long-term, serious relationship can really cramp his style. Peter Pan likes being with you—but only sometimes, not all of the time.

Unfortunately, you can't force him into a commitment. You may find yourself giving him an ultimatum, but, before you do, decide what you really want from him. What kind of relationship makes you happy, and can this guy really provide it? He might eventually commit to you. The question is, how long do you want to wait?

The Family Guy

You'll recognize the Family Guy right away. He's probably a great uncle to his niece or nephew and definitely wants to have a family of his own. He tries to date women who are serious about eventually having a family and doesn't really date around. He probably has a plan for finding and wooing the right woman, and already knows when he'll be ready to get married.

A lot of women don't believe the Family Guy exists, but he does. The key is catching him while he's still single. Obviously, he's more ready than other men for commitment. With him, you have to make sure that *you* are ready for the kind of commitment *he* wants! Take your time and really get to know him so you don't get more caught up in the notion of getting married than you are in making sure he's the right guy.

The Eternal Playboy

This man enjoys the company of women, but really steers clear of committing to one. These men weren't raised on the relationship fantasy, they were taught to run from it. These are the guys who give the men who want a relationship a bad name. When it comes to commitment, the Eternal Playboy looks the other way. There are a number of reasons why: He could be completely irresponsible, or just really enjoys the attention of multiple women.

Interestingly enough, even the Eternal Playboy can get hung up on one woman. She just has to really be the right woman for him. Dating him can be a challenge, so if you're going to be that special woman who finally breaks this wild stallion, be sure you know exactly what you want from him. Chasing the Eternal Playboy can be exhausting, so know up front whether you're ready for the challenge.

The Go-with-the-Flow Guy

This guy is neither a commitment-phobe nor a serious marrying man. He just finds a woman he likes and stays with her. He's probably open to getting married, but would be content just living together—you know, whatever.

If you find yourself dating this guy, you have to know what kind of commitment will make *you* happiest, because he won't be making the call. There are a lot of men who don't get caught up in things having to be a certain way. As long as your relationship is stress-free, this guy's going to be fine with it. If things move naturally, then anything goes—but it will be up to you to help drive it.

Find the Balance to Make You Both Happy

Women get caught up in the emotions of a relationship. They think that if the feelings are there, it can always work, so they're always more open to making a relationship last. On the other hand, men will be in a relationship with you, but if you're not what they think of as their ideal, the relationship is going nowhere. Men can be detached with their feelings so they can walk away easily if they're not getting what they want. In some instances, men and women will stay in a relationship just because they're used to it, even if neither of them are happy. How do you meet in the middle so that both people get what they want? How do you get involved without getting hurt?

Relationships can be challenging. The reality is that meeting someone you want to be with is only half the battle. It is hard to find the perfect balance where both people are giving 100 percent and feeling happy all of the time. Sometimes you will give 80 percent while he's giving 20. Other times you'll be giving 10 percent and he is giving 90. The bigger challenge is for both of you to be committed, prepared for the hard exercises, and both always fighting for the same side. You have to get through the drills and do the work to have your relationship be victorious.

Unfortunately, there's no single, correct way. The best place to start is to be honest with one another and find the best way to communicate so you are on the same page. Talk to your guy to understand what he thinks about the type of commitment you are seeking. You'll be better able to see what your relationship may be facing down the road. If you know what is important to one another, you can begin to relate as a couple, not as two individuals trying to have their way. Here are some things you can do to help your relationship move in the right direction:

♡ Do not try to make your relationship about "us time" all the time. Establish couple days and individual days so you have time to be together and time to pursue things separately.

♡ You don't have to spend every waking moment together. Give yourselves a chance to miss each other.

♡ Let him do some of the pursuing. Even in a relationship, men get tired of the mundane. Don't always be the one to call him.

♡ When you have a disagreement, let him come to you. You have a better chance of solving a problem when both of you are receptive. Address issues when you're both ready to be levelheaded.

♡ Talk about your pet peeves and hang-ups. Be open about what you're both dealing with, so it doesn't pop up as a surprise or petty argument later.

♡ Don't lose yourself in the relationship—remember that you are still an individual. Be yourself and still do the things you enjoy, alone or with friends and family members.

♡ Establish boundaries. Let him know if you have a problem with him dropping by without calling first.

♡ Make it clear to him that you're not trying to take over or run his life, and you don't want him to do that to yours.

Maintain Control

Maintain control in how you interact with your new guy. If you establish early on that you are emotionally needy, he will probably back away. If you're confident and self-assured, then he'll treat you that way. You have to train him to treat you the way you want to be treated. Don't give him a reason to run from you. Instead, give him a reason to want to be around you. Make it clear to him that you don't expect him to replace all of the other priorities in your life. Be your normal, go-getter self and make him a supplement to your life, not a replacement.

Maintaining control is important, because how you interact now will set the tone for your relationship. Give him just enough information to keep him interested and keep the rest under your hat until it is the right time to reveal more.

Take It as It Comes

As in dating, you cannot rush your significant other down the aisle just because you are in a relationship. Let the relationship take the time it needs. Some relationships lead to marriage; others just end. You won't know where yours is going until it gets there.

Taking time to enjoy every step is important. The more you get to know your significant other, the more it will become clear if you really have met a life partner. This may take a year, or it make take several. Either way, taking it slow now will help you know if you have the kind of relationship that can survive.

Make It Happen!

Establish positive communication with your partner early in your relationship. If you do, you will have a better chance to have open discussions about any topic.

Don't ...

- Expect everything between you two to be perfect.
- Force the relationship to progress faster than it needs to.
- Base your relationship on what you see in your friends' situations.

206

Do ...

- Enjoy all the moments of your relationship.

- Learn as much as you can about your partner so you will know if he is a good fit for the long run.

- Take time to learn the good, bad, and ugly about your partner.

- Have open talks about what you both want to ensure you are on the same page.

Avoid the Full Monty

After being single, a relationship can bring a certain level of comfort to any woman. Your man is wonderful to be around, fun to talk to, and he likes to share with you. Be careful, though, that you don't share too much too soon. As an old adage reminds us, "Some things are better kept to oneself."

It's great that you feel free enough to want to tell him anything. If he's becoming your best friend, eventually you'll probably tell him more about yourself than you've ever told anyone. But keep in mind that, in the early stages, he is getting to know you and still learning what he likes and dislikes. Don't sabotage yourself and tell him all the good and bad right away.

However, if there are things that you think may be an issue for the two of you, get it out of the way early. For example, if you already know that it is hard for you to have overnight guests as a single parent, be up front about it. Or if you don't want to include him in certain areas of your life, let him know. Tell him early on if you have an illness that causes you to be hospitalized from time to time, or that your family is really close-knit and they drop by all the time. Don't waste your time with someone who can't understand or handle certain things about you. It's better to be candid than have a situation develop that you could have addressed earlier.

Drill Sergeant Says ...

You don't have to tell your new partner everything about yourself right away, but there are some things you should talk about. By this time, you hopefully have discussed ...

- Your parenting status or co-parenting situation.
- Whether or not you have a chronic illness.
- If you're *truly* single.
- Any unconventional traits, such as living in a commune.
- Deal-breakers, such as not wanting to have children.

Don't Get Swept Away

If you've been single and haven't been with anyone special in a long time, it may be really easy to swoon over this new guy. He has all of these great qualities, he's cute, and he's all yours! Before the feeling starts running away with you, keep in mind that you just got him. It's okay to have those lovin' feelings, but keep them in perspective. You may be setting yourself up for disaster.

If you get swept away by your feelings too early, you may get frustrated if he doesn't immediately seem to feel the same. Questions like, "How do you feel about me?" and "Do you love me?" start coming way before it's time. You want your feelings to grow out of genuine emotion, not from infatuation. You also don't want him to think you're moving too fast and not giving him a chance to let his feelings grow. He might think you're trying to rush him to the altar and run.

Make It Happen!

Don't put too much pressure on your guy too early. Keep him interested, don't overwhelm him.

Don't ...

- Tell him all of your deep feelings for him when it's only been a short time; he may feel overwhelmed and pull away.
- Expect him to feel the way you do right away.
- Pressure him into getting his feelings up to speed with yours.

continues

continued

Do ...

- Monitor your feelings. Are you falling for him, or just falling?

- Wait at least a few months before you share your more intense feelings.

- Use your girlfriend support network for sharing and insight.

- Write your feelings in a journal.

- Tell him how you feel after you've had a chance to really get to know him.

Solidify Your Relationship Status

Laylah met Danny over the Internet and they immediately clicked. They dated and spent a lot of time together. Laylah assumed that Danny considered her his girlfriend, especially when he started referring to her by pet names and inviting her over all the time. There seemed to be nothing that Danny wouldn't do for her; he even made comments about Laylah meeting his mother and friends. Even so, when Laylah got comfortable enough to call Danny her boyfriend, he became distant and weird.

*Eventually Laylah confronted Danny, and he told
her he wasn't interested in anything serious at that
time. Laylah felt hurt and confused, and doesn't
understand to this day what happened.*

You know what happened. Laylah didn't ask for clarification
and assumed too much about her status with Danny. Back
in the day, when a gentleman was interested in a lady, he
would first court her to make his intentions known. He
would ask for her parents' or another relative's approval,
and then he would ask her to officially be his "steady girl"
or whatever term signified their relationship.

Times have changed, and now women are lucky to have
a man ask her to be his girlfriend. Women have to be careful
here. With the looseness of dating and relationship parameters, a woman might think she and her man are involved
exclusively, while he sees her as just another girl he spends
time with.

It almost seems silly for adults to refer to one another
as "boyfriend" and "girlfriend"; however, you need some
way to establish what kind of relationship you're in. If
you're close enough to be physically intimate with him, you
should be able to ask him what type of relationship you
are involved in. Ask sooner rather than later so you know
if you are where you want to be with him.

> **Drill Sergeant Says ...**
>
> Avoid making one of the most fatal relationship *faux pas* that women make. Lots of woman go with the flow and assume that a man is her boyfriend when he really doesn't want to be committed and just isn't telling her. Be clear about what you want from the relationship in the early stages. Go ahead and ask the hard question: "What are we calling this relationship?" More clarification up front will keep you from being disappointed later.

If a man refers to you as his girl or indicates somehow that you have a special status, do not assume. Men are still slow to commit and feel pressured when women push too much. Even if it seems like he's on the same page, it's better to ask. If he's ready for an exclusive relationship, he'll be forthright and nothing will change. However, if he's wishy-washy about committing, it's better for you to know now. He could be actively dating while you are thinking exclusivity. In addition, you really want to know what is going on, especially if you are being intimate with him. Remember, it is always better to be safe than sorry.

Introducing Him to Significant People

Unfortunately, relationships are not just about the two people involved. If you're planning to have a long-term relationship, your significant other will eventually meet and interact with the other significant people in your life. Some of them will be completely receptive to him, while others might have some kind of issue with him.

When you introduce your man to people who are important to you, hope for the best and expect the worst. It's easy to assume that most people will be immediately receptive to you and your partner as a couple, but sometimes people are just used to seeing you as an individual. Everyone involved loves you and only wants the best for you. So, when an outsider comes in and takes up your affection and attention, the people who care are going to be on guard. They will find a way to learn more about him, understand his intentions, and see if he is as great as he seems to be with you. It may feel like he is meeting the firing squad, because all of them will size him up in their own way.

Your man should be able to understand and handle it, but it is still your job to try to make the introductions as smooth as possible. Ultimately, it's your decision to be with this man, but it is important to try to help everyone get along for the long haul. The key to understanding and acceptance is to consider the feelings of everyone involved. Eventually, everybody will get used to each other and it will seem like your significant other has been there all along.

Meeting Your Friends

Your friends have probably been hearing about this guy from the first moment he stepped in front of you. They're excited, curious, anxious, and skeptical. Depending on how many close friends you have, it may be quite a hurdle for him to impress everyone. Take the pressure off both sides by utilizing the following tips:

♡ Meet in a relaxed environment, such as a sports bar or jazz lounge.

♡ Tell your friends as much as you can about him so they know enough to start a conversation without "grilling" him.

♡ In turn, tell your beau enough about your friends so he's not meeting them without crib notes.

♡ Be the conversation referee. If you feel things are going down the wrong road and getting too personal or negative, change the subject.

♡ Show solidarity with your mate by sitting or standing close to him.

♡ Have a set time for the evening to end so there's no awkwardness, especially if the night is not going well.

♡ Try to end the evening on a high note by saying something positive about everyone.

Meeting Your Children

Having your significant other meet your children is a crucial step. Your kids will always come first, but you have to make him feel important. Your children may immediately have an issue with another man stepping in where their father might have been. Help everyone get along by implementing some of the following suggestions:

♡ Meet somewhere fun so the entire interaction with your new man is not just about meeting him.

♡ Explain to your children that no one is replacing their father, and he will always have that role with them.

♡ Position your new man as a friend and someone to get to know—that's all. Keep the scope of his role neutral until the kids feel comfortable having him around.

♡ Talk to your kids after the meeting to give them an opportunity to tell you how they really feel.

♡ Don't have your significant other take on a parenting role until you're certain that your relationship is on its way toward marriage.

♡ Remember that this is awkward for everyone. Keep interactions light. Don't force the kids and your man to be instant friends; let them come around in their own way.

Meeting Your Parents

Introducing your significant other to your parents is another big step. Your parents love you and only want the best for you. They'll have your beau under a microscope from the first handshake. The firing of questions cannot be helped, but you can ensure that your man doesn't feel attacked. Mediate with the following tips:

♡ Take him to meet your parents at their home, don't meet in yours. That way you can leave whenever you need to. Plan to keep it fairly short.

♡ Tell your parents tidbits about your significant other, and arm your significant other with some history on your parents.

♡ Establish a code word so that if things get hairy, you can shuffle your beau off to look at your childhood swing set, outside. Use a word like "smog" or "butter-fly"; you can easily use it in a sentence to throw your parents off.

♡ If you're not in the midst of planning your wedding, then don't let your parents start planning it! If they try to push that conversation on you, politely change the subject.

Is There Ever a Right Time?

There is no perfect time to introduce your significant other to the important people in your life, but in this one area it's best to do it later rather than sooner. If your relationship is still relatively new, wait to show him around until you're sure he's going to *stay* around.

If you've been dating for a while, think about why it is important for you to introduce him to your inner circle. Do you feel certain that he's going to be in your life as a semi-permanent fixture? Or do you just want to show him off? Think carefully about this; you don't want to have your worlds collide fruitlessly.

Especially take more time when introducing him to your children. Children have expectations and get attached to people very easily. You don't want to have to explain why Mommy had to make their new best buddy go away.

Use your best judgment to determine the best time for your beau to meet everyone. If you have any reservations, then hold off. If your guy is going to be around a while, there will be *lots* of opportunities.

13

The Sex Guide

Sex is one of those things that you don't expect to be questioned about as an adult. When you're in a relationship, most people won't question what you do or when you do it. However, their perceptions may change slightly when you're not in a long-term relationship and you're dating more than one person.

In the final stages of your boot camp training, your Drill Sergeant helps you explore the many aspects of single sex. Also, she will assist you with overcoming any hang-ups that other people may have. As a trained field operative, only you can make the final decision on whether what you're doing is right or wrong.

Sex and the Dating Woman

American society has a love-hate relationship with sex. Everyone knows that everyone is doing it, but the media handles sex in a strange way. Couples can make love on soap operas during daytime television, but you rarely see people having sex as passionately on evening television unless it is late at night. Adults talk to one another about sex, but they have to be careful where they talk about it. It's taboo at work, in certain social venues, or in some social circles.

Sex is a natural, physical act that no one should be ashamed of, but people can easily make it something shameful. Even though people speak more openly about sex than they used to, some prudish stigmas still affect single women today. If a man is dating and having sexual relations with various women, he might just be considered a cool guy playing the field.

However, if a woman is doing the same, some consider her loose or fast. Some people even say that if a woman hasn't married by her mid-30s, she just wants to hang out and be a playgirl. Just because a woman chooses to date doesn't mean that she's having sex with everybody. And even if she is, so what? She's an adult making her own choices; why should anyone else be concerned? As long as she is honest with the men she is involved with, no one else should judge her.

Drill Sergeant Says ...

Dating can become complicated with sex. Whether you're dating one person or a few, you should be honest with the men you're involved with. Even if you're looking for a long-term relationship, you decide whether or not to keep sex out of the formula or have casual sex in all of your relationships. Either way, be honest and considerate of other people's feelings, and always practice safe sex.

Helen invited Sheila to a holiday barbecue. Sheila had been single for some time and was openly dating. At the barbecue, Sheila met Helen's friend, Mike. Sheila went on a few dates with Mike and became intimate with him. Weeks later, Helen and Sheila met for lunch. Helen was shocked to learn that Sheila had not only been intimate with Mike, but was having an intimate relationship with another man at the same time. Sheila couldn't understand why Helen was so upset with her. If she were a guy, Helen wouldn't give her such a hard time.

What's good for the gander is still not good for the goose by society's standards. However, if you're a single, dating woman, it's your decision whether you want to have sex with the men you're dating. No one else is going to determine what you do behind closed doors except you and your partner. One single woman may choose not to be intimate with the men she is dating; another may decide that she wants that level of intimacy with everyone she dates.

Of course, it's also up to you to deal with the consequences that being intimate can bring to your relationship. Whether you are intimate with one date or many, there are pros and cons to bringing this level of intimacy into a relationship. The following table lists some of these.

Having Sex: The Pros and Cons

Pros	Cons
Sex is a natural, physical act.	You have to be cautious with whom you have sex.
You set the parameters of what type of sexual relationship you want to have.	You have to be careful—have safe sex and be in safe situations.
It feels good; why not?	Being safe does not always protect you from disease or pregnancy.
If you can start, you can stop.	Sex changes things and it is not always easy to get out of a relationship with a more physical aspect.
You are not getting emotionally involved.	To the contrary, both men and women can get emotionally attached when having a sexual relationship.

Even as adults, women still have to face the fact that being in a sexual relationship doesn't always bring out the adult in the men they date. If you let a man you're dating know you're having a sexual relationship with someone else while you're sleeping with him, he may not be completely understanding. On the same note, a man may say he's okay with this, and then become possessive and unruly, trying to gain all of your attention. In the worst-case scenario, he may get so irate that he'll either want to cut it off with you or physically injure the other guy.

On the other hand, let's say that you choose to not tell anyone that you are intimately involved with more than one man. Can you divide your attention between two or more men this way? If you're intimate with one and not with another, will you begin to favor one more than the other? Are you being fair to the men you're involved with by not being honest? Finally, can you truly be involved with more than one person when sex is involved?

These are good questions to ask yourself. Things can get complicated and it may get hard to determine what kind of relationships you are having. Find out what really works for you. Only you can determine what works for you.

How Intimate Should You Be?

If you have an intimate relationship with someone you are dating, you also have to determine how intimate you want to be. Is kissing and heavy petting enough, or do you want more of a sexual relationship? There are many forms of intimacy; determine what's best for you and your relationship.

Drill Sergeant Says ...

There are no rules about determining how intimate you should be with the person that you're dating. Only you and your partner can decide what is appropriate for you both.

It is helpful to realize your boundaries before you get down the path and are uncertain of what you want. You have to determine what you feel comfortable with and at what stage you want more intimacy in your relationship. In some cases, you may want to be more intimate, and in others maybe not. It depends on you and what you want out of the relationships you are formulating.

Make It Happen!

How do you determine when your interaction is taking a turn to becoming more involved? Take a look at the chart below to determine what level of intimacy you are experiencing in your relationships:

Kissing (simple peck)	Casual interaction
Kissing (French kissing)	Borderline casual and more involved
Light Petting	Borderline casual interaction/more involved

More Intimate Petting	Getting a little more serious
Very Intimate Petting	More involved/ very involved
All the Way	Very involved interaction

Before you decide to have a more intimate relationship, know what you are getting into. The man you are involved with should respect and understand how you feel when it comes to what degree you are intimate with him. Take your time to figure it out; don't feel pressured to get involved if you don't want to. Remember, you are in control of your body.

Determine When It's Okay to Engage

Once you determine what levels of intimacy you are comfortable with, the next big question is, how do you know when you should? It's not an easy question to answer. Sometimes it's not about the level of your relationship, but about what is going on with you. Maybe you just want to experience certain levels of intimacy without getting too hung up on timing. Maybe you want to wait until you feel comfortable to get involved with the right person. Take a look at your circumstances and determine your next move.

Before you get involved, think about your current circumstances. Is this the best time to have a sexual relationship with someone? Or is it better to keep it less complicated while you are dating? Or do you feel that you would get emotionally involved and you are not sure if this is what you want? Whatever the case, take some time to think through the whole scenario before you act.

It's Been a Long Time

Sometimes it just might be necessary for you to get your groove on. There's nothing wrong with feeling this way. If you're dating someone you feel comfortable with, and you practice safe sex, then go for it!

However, it may be good to think about what type of relationship you have with your potential sex partner. If you and your partner are on the same page, then everything should be fine. If you're not seeing eye-to-eye on your relationship status, you may want to ask yourself a few questions. Will you be able to deal with the relationship not working out if you are intimate? If you're not that interested in him, will you be able to walk away after you engage sexually?

Think through what kind of relationship you have with him and determine if he is the best candidate for an intimate interlude.

You Want It to Be the Right Time

Sometimes it's better to hold off until the right moment. Maybe a special, romantic evening will turn intimate. Maybe you want to wait and see where the relationship is going before you get involved physically. Maybe you've hit a relationship milestone and would like to take it to the next level. Whatever the case, holding out for the right moment can make your lovemaking session one to remember.

The Build-Up Has Been Hot and Heavy

What do you do when the intensity between two people just keeps getting more intense? You can either keep letting it build, or you can do something about it. Physical attraction is hard to ignore; it rears up in even the most nonchalant interactions. If you choose not to do anything about it, you and your date will probably continue to grow more and more uncomfortable around one another. The flirting will continue to build until you can barely handle standing near one another. If you do give in, you can bet you'll have a wild affair!

The biggest thing to be cautious of is that something like this, built up over time, can result in a few great sexual encounters, but will rarely develop into a meaningful relationship. If you're prepared for the intense lovemaking sessions and can handle it if nothing else develops, then go for it!

The Kids Are Away, Mommy Can Play

It's usually frowned upon for a single parent with children to date and have sex. However, mothers are adults, too, and shouldn't feel ashamed to want to engage in an intimate situation with someone. The key is to not involve your children with this man until you're really sure how you would like to deal with him yourself.

If you decide to become intimate, enlist a babysitter for the evening or send your kids to visit a relative and go to his house. There's nothing wrong with being involved; you just don't want to entangle your kids in your romantic involvements. Be an adult, have fun, and practice safe sex.

What Kind of Relationship Are You In?

You know you want to get intimate with this man, but how do you know your relationship can handle it? The best way to figure this out is to have a good handle on what type of relationship you have in the first place.

Sure, you're dating, but you may not have established what type of relationship you have with this man. If you're in doubt, don't make assumptions about your status. Have a real talk—*outside* of any sexual context—and make sure you're both on the same page.

What kind of relationship are you establishing? Think about it and determine whether or not your interaction is ready to deal with sexual considerations.

Just Friends

In the early stages of dating, friendship is a good foundation to have. Even if he's taking you out on dates and you think you are more than a date, sometimes you're still at the "just friends" level until more intimacy is introduced. If you haven't even had a goodnight kiss, you're not going to be jumping in the sack right away. If you want more, you may have to hold out a little longer.

If you're fine with a slowly evolving relationship, then don't introduce sex into it. You can let him guide the levels of intimacy and wait for the first kiss, or you can kiss him. Either way, intimacy will be a slow build; as long as you're okay with it, you may have the makings of something more special.

Dating with Strong Attraction

When there's a spark, there is fire. When you're dating someone you're attracted to, it's hard to put strong parameters on when you will get intimate. It could happen any time! When two people are attracted to one another, that attraction can overtake the situation.

The question is whether or not this is a long-term relationship. In the early stages, it's hard to tell. Throwing sex in too soon can make or break a new relationship, but if you're open to the experience, sex can be good with someone you're just comfortable with and attracted to.

If you're looking for something more, you may want to be clear on where your relationship is before you introduce sex. If you both feel like you have a good relationship in the making, a deeper level of intimacy can also bring the two of you closer.

> **Drill Sergeant Says ...**
>
> No matter what the stage of your relationship, you and your partner should be on the same page so you both know what to expect. Communicate openly and honestly about whether or not you are both ready to take your relationship to another level.

All Systems Go

If you've established that you're in a full-fledged relationship, and you haven't been intimate, sex becomes the next logical step. You can still take things slow and build up to a sexual encounter. Keep in mind, being intimate within a relationship is still about you being comfortable. Don't move into something sexual until you are ready. Even though you're now involved, don't let the momentum of the relationship push you into sex until you both want it.

If it has taken time for you to be intimate, don't rush it for the sake of being intimate. You're not on a timetable. On the other hand, if you're both ready, then appreciate being on the same page. Even within a relationship, take the same precautions and practice safe sex.

Sex Changes Things

Sandy had been going out with Tim for about a month. They were attracted to one another and often spoke about being intimate. One night, they took their relationship to the next level and had sex. Sandy didn't think their relationship would be negatively affected, but she prepared herself for a good or bad result. After their sexual interlude, Sandy and Tim continued to date and their relationship became more serious.

No matter where your relationship is, realize that sex will change the dynamic. The key is being able to deal with how your relationship may change for the better or worse. When you become intimate, you're sharing yourself on a deeper level. Hopefully, you and your partner are ready to experience something deeper and you'll both have similar feelings, but be prepared for any fallout that having sex may create if you don't.

Even when you think things are going to go well, sometimes men freak out, thinking that since you had sex you will have higher expectations from them. Men typically think that women develop a stronger emotional tie to someone they're having sex with and cannot have a detached sexual affair.

Think about where you are in your relationship, and don't expect the relationship to change into something more than it is immediately afterwards. If you're realistic along these lines, you'll be less likely to be hurt.

Drill Sergeant Says ...

Be ready to deal with the consequences of being intimate with your partner. If you're not sure you could deal with him not continuing the relationship afterwards, you should give it more time and thought before being sexual.

You have the power to have a sexual relationship or not. You also have the ability to accept the encounter as simply an experience you shared with someone you like. In some cases, the experience can mean more to you and your partner in a positive way. Sex is powerful and brings deeper feelings into your relationship.

Sex can be shared on many different levels with whom you are involved. Be sure to think through how it will affect your relationship.

Sex can be a ...

♡ **Casual fun experience:** No ties, more than likely won't affect your interaction.

♡ **Next step in interaction:** Reflection of how you both feel in your relationship. Can make your relationship grow into more or not.

♡ **Deeply engaging:** Very intimate, can make a deeper connection and more than likely will.

♡ **Soul-stirring moment:** Both feel the earth move; probably more than just good sex happening here.

14

Keeping It Going

You're able to control nearly every other area in your life, so why are relationships so hard? It's simple, really: relationships involve another person. It would be great to have a man stand at attention while you shout orders and then watch him do what you want, when you want.

Unfortunately, it doesn't work that way. Relationships aren't about someone doing exactly what you want them to do. Relationships are about two people coming together through understanding and compromise.

You can't always tell if a relationship is going to work, but you can do your best to try to make it work. Still, even with your best efforts, you may find yourself looking at a failed relationship. Don't blame yourself. Maybe you both had similar interests, but then your interests changed and you started growing apart. Maybe you never wanted the same things. Maybe it was just bad timing.

Take your focus away from the relationship and focus on you. The sooner you're okay with it, the sooner you can put your helmet back on, repack your gear, and get back into the field. You won't win every battle, but there are always more lands to conquer.

Dealing with a Bad Date or Breakup

It stinks when things don't go the way you expected, but remember that you're not in combat alone. If your partner's having a bad day, it can spill over into your interaction. If you were frustrated with your last conversation, that feeling can creep over into your next date. It would be nice if we could deal with each area of our lives independently, but soldiers aren't robots, so you can't just compartmentalize things.

Your interactions with each other aren't always going to be positive. It's best to be with someone who understands you, your moods, and your life, and can at least keep things constructive. When you're with someone who's more likely to escalate negativity than defuse it, things can go badly very quickly. It might be best to cut your losses and scout out a person who is a better fit.

The Funky Date

> *Rose couldn't wait to see Roger all week. They had busy schedules, so it had been three weeks since their last date. Rose made sure she looked great and wore the perfume that Roger bought her. But when Roger came to pick her up, he was clearly irritated. Rose kept asking him what was wrong and he kept grumbling, "Nothing." Roger's attitude continued throughout the date. Needless to say, Rose didn't enjoy dinner. In fact, she couldn't wait to get back home.*

There's nothing more frustrating than having a date you thought would be great turn out bad. You looked all week for the right outfit, got your hair done, and pulled together your accessories—then your date is a jerk the whole night and all your anticipation goes out the window.

The first thing to recognize is that it was just a date: You're not curing cancer or building a rocket. It was supposed to be a fun evening to get to know this man better. A bad date is still just a date, and that doesn't have to define your entire interaction with this person.

Make It Happen!

Before you start making excuses and blaming yourself, evaluate what happened:

- Was your date in a bad mood?
- Were you in a bad mood?
- Did either of you bring some negativity from your day into your interaction?
- Was there some residual funkiness from a previous interaction between the two of you?

Think about how these things could have contributed to your bad date, then consider whether the two of you can get past it or if you'll have another date at all. If you think you can get past it, let it go and start fresh. If not, chalk it up to a bad fit. Remember, he's just one fish in the sea. Take it in stride and make plans with someone else!

Life happens, and a bad date can merely be a reflection of what's going on with you or your partner at that moment. It's not necessarily indicative of your whole relationship. Sometimes, however, a bad date can highlight serious issues in the relationship.

If this is the first time you saw this guy, it may be safe to say that he's not the best fit for you. Anyone can have a bad day, but if he wasn't willing to put on his best face for his first date with you, then he's probably not a good candidate for a longer-term commitment. If you've been seeing him for a while, then put it in context and analyze what went on. Are your interactions usually this funky? Is there always something that comes up and keeps ruining your dates?

The Bad Breakup

Patrice thought her relationship was great even though she and Adam argued frequently. When Adam told her it was over, she couldn't understood why. Instead, she cried and pleaded with him to stay and make it work, which only made him pull away even more. After the dust settled, Patrice thought about some of the major issues in their relationship. Adam had never seemed to have time for dates after he started his new job. He worked all the time and seemed irritated whenever Patrice asked about getting together.

Patrice realized it would have taken a lot of effort on both their parts to maintain a relationship he had no time for. Patrice felt bad about the loss, but, in the end, she knew it was for the best.

No matter how long you have been going out, breakups are never pleasant. A lot of women see a breakup in only one way: "Failure!" Once again you have lost the battle.

Change your perspective on this: A breakup means something wasn't working. It's easy to get lost in the emotions of breaking up, wondering why you couldn't make it work, why you couldn't try harder. These thoughts are valid, but only to a point. Sometimes two people just aren't a good fit. Why waste your time pining over something that wasn't going to bring you joy? Instead, be proud of yourself for recognizing what you need and refusing to settle for less.

Women tend to focus on what *could be* instead of what *is*. If you were compatible, then would you have broken up or would you have worked it out? Were you trying to ignore the obvious signs that something was wrong? Marching lock-step in a relationship, you often fail to see the land mines. However, if there are problems you're not dealing with, they're probably going to explode sooner or later.

Make It Happen!

No one feels good after a breakup, no matter what the reasons. Feel the pain, assess the damage, and take no prisoners!

Don't ...

- Spend too much time being emotional about the breakup. The more emotional energy you expend, the harder it will be to get back to normal.

- Let this breakup turn you into a prisoner of war. Your feelings were hurt, but don't let this break you.

- Play the blame game. Finding fault won't change the situation.

- Get together with your platoon-mates for a pity party.

- Identify your dating life with this one bad dating moment.

Do ...

- Acknowledge what happened and review what could have been different. Note things you can improve, revise your battle plan, and then let it go.

- Give yourself some love: Buy a pair of shoes, spend some girlfriend time, or get a massage.

- Lean on your friends in a positive way: Have a relationship-ending party, a road trip, or a good-riddance martini toast.

- Get back into the field. Get out there and meet men who are a better fit!

Breakups are hard and it's okay for your feelings to be hurt. Acknowledge what happened, but don't dwell on it; it only prolongs the pain for no good reason. Take time to regroup,but don't rehash the negative feelings. Instead, take time just feeling better about you. Eliminate blame and the "shoulda-woulda-coulda's." It happened; work through your feelings and get over it.

Drill Sergeant Says ...

Breakups always threaten to undo all the work you've done to improve yourself. Don't slide backward! Think about all the progress you've made: a new, positive attitude, weight loss, or more social confidence. Don't let a setback make you feel bad about yourself, and don't bear all the blame for a situation that, after all, involved two people. Love yourself and let it go.

Learning the Lessons

After the heat of battle, you probably want to hide in your barracks and eat a gallon of ice cream. If it'll make you feel better, do it, but don't kid yourself that it'll change what happened. Don't dwell on the bad incident; focus on the underlying causes of what happened.

Some men are notorious for making women feel bad about something they did or something you both created.

They attack your self-esteem and make you feel bad about yourself. If you already feel bad about yourself, it's easy for you to believe you're to blame.

Don't let this happen. If the negative tape is still running through your head, hit the stop button. The sooner you stop feeling bad, the sooner you'll find positive takeaways from the situation. Even if the situation seems to be all about him, there are still things that you can learn so you don't end up here again. Did you …

♡ Push for things to only be your way?

♡ Give him too much power over your time and needs?

♡ Expect more than he was able or willing to give?

♡ Put too much pressure on making the relationship something it wasn't?

♡ Allow him to pressure you too much?

♡ Wait for him to make things better?

♡ Put your life on hold until things changed between you?

♡ Fail to see compromises you could have made to make it work?

Whatever the circumstances, there is always something to learn about yourself. Maybe next time you'll be more aware of the early warning signs that things aren't working out. Or maybe next time you won't immediately jump to blaming yourself for the demise of the relationship.

Don't pine over what you've lost when you have so much more to gain. In your next relationship, you'll be smarter about what you need and what he needs to make it work, and you won't waste your energies trying to save a sinking ship.

After you acknowledge and learn the lessons, you won't bring the same issues into your next relationship. Taking time now will save you from repeating the same lessons next time around.

Pulling Yourself Back Together

Your focus right now should be on you. Bad relationships and breakups take energy away from you, and can even prevent you from seeing all the good things you have. Remember, what happened was just one incident and does not reflect everything else in your life. You've come a long way in your training. You can't let one setback define your whole dating outlook. It is now in the past. Be strong, soldier! Take back your power and rebuild yourself!

You only lost a battle, you haven't lost the war. You have all the tools you need to get back out there. Add these mental weapons to your tool kit.

You're Still the Same Person

Isn't it funny how so many of the things men say they like about you in the beginning are the things they say they don't like about you in the end? You're still the same person he thought was so great before. Just because it didn't work out doesn't mean you have to go on a crusade to become something different.

Be who you are and don't change because a potential relationship didn't work out. You just need to find a better fit, not morph yourself to fit into his world.

Think About Your Needs

You may not think so, but the best time to re-evaluate your needs is right after a failed situation. You have a realistic view of what you're looking for and can see what's truly important to you.

You may have thought that dating someone with a high-powered career would be great, but now you've learned that such men are often not around to be in a relationship, because they're always off doing high-powered career-type stuff. Think about the profile of the man you seek and factor in qualities that may not have seemed as important before.

It's All Trial and Error

Don't throw in the towel after just one bad situation. The more you date, the closer you'll get to what you want. If there was a straightforward formula to finding the right man, then every woman would have her perfect man and there wouldn't be so many songs about love gone bad.

Unfortunately, you're going to kiss a few toads before you land your prince. What's more, even when you find him, he's not going to be as perfect as you think he should be. After all, he's only human, just like you! The only way to improve your odds is to get up, dust yourself off, and get back out there.

Nothing Ventured, Nothing Gained

Maybe you're reading this and thinking, once again, that this is a lot of work. Well, what that brings great rewards isn't? The athlete who wins an Olympic gold medal is probably tired, beat-up, and sore by the time she gets her hands on the medal. Anyone who's ever made any kind of major accomplishment will tell you that it was hell along the way.

Getting what you want can be hard. The key is to recognize that it doesn't have to be *emotionally* difficult. Look at things from a different perspective. You encountered a bad situation, but hey, instead of sitting home alone and dateless, at least you were out there. Any positive actions you're taking now are only getting you closer to the wonderful man you're looking for. Keep making the effort and you will be rewarded.

Get Back Out There and Feel Good About It

So you're ready to get back out there again. Great! Look at this as another opportunity to get what you want. All those escapades with the ones who didn't work out were not in vain. All of your interactions with men help you to zero in on what you really want and need in a mate and a relationship.

You should feel good about where you are: You're back in the arena and ahead of the game, with skills that set you apart from the competition. You're still single, but you're not in a bad relationship, locked into something that isn't right for you. You're in the right place to get what you want, so go for it!

Things didn't work out this time, but you're getting closer to what you want. Now that you have more field experience, you will be more effective. This is what your training is all about; the more you have, the more experienced you will be. What follows are some more positive perspectives.

Closer Than Close

You are so close to getting what you want, don't feel bad. You are on the path to getting the right man and the kind of relationship that you want. You know more about your needs and you're not going back to getting a man just to say you have a boyfriend. Stay diligent, and you'll be able to wade through the men you don't want straight to the man you do.

You Never Have to Settle

Don't feel bad if the last situation didn't work out. Men are like buses—there's always another one around the corner. Women waste too much energy thinking there's only one great man for them and if they haven't met him yet, he won't come. He's out there—hundreds of him—so you don't have to just take whoever comes your way. If you know what you want, then keep expecting to get it.

Have Your Cake and Eat It, Too

You have to believe that you can have what you want and be happy. There's no reason for you not to have the man you want and the relationship you've longed for. It doesn't have to be a fantasy—it can be as real as you want it to be.

Recognize and Maintain a Real Relationship

When you do find that great relationship you're seeking, will you be able to recognize it? You have to look at where you've been to know where you're going. By learning from past situations and being clear on what you are willing to accept, you'll be ready to be a part of a functioning and healthy relationship.

Women put a lot of energy into dreaming the perfect guy, but not a whole lot into envisioning the relationship they want. Once you have the guy, you have to make your relationship last. It's not easy, but you can have a good relationship. If you work on it together, you'll have the relationship you desire for a lifetime.

Know What It Takes

Relationships aren't always about candy and flowers. If you go into a relationship believing they are, it is doomed to fail. Sure, having a great relationship is about the good stuff, but it's more important to be able to get through the hard times together.

The key is being on the same page with your desires and supporting each other's needs. It sounds good, but it's not always easy. Why do you think married people always tell you that the grass is not always greener? Merging your life with someone else's is hard. You're sharing your space, your time, and maybe even some of your independence. It's not always fun. It takes growth and maturity from both you and your partner. However, if you both want it and have built a good foundation, you can work through these changes together.

Every couple has disagreements, but really delve into what is at the core of a given argument. Certain topics are hard to deal with, such as finances, child rearing, in-laws, lack of couple time, and managing each other's expectations. Most people have the argument and barely agree to disagree.

Find out what's really keeping you two in opposite corners. Does your partner think you're not listening to him? Do you feel that he doesn't give you a voice on certain topics? Does he really know what is important to you? Do you give him room to make mistakes and learn from them? None of these questions are easy to answer, but the answers will help you gain the mutual respect and understanding that you need so you can deal with the tough issues.

By being supportive and understanding toward one another, you can conquer any obstacles that come your way. Together, you can make your relationship a lasting one.

Understand Your Level of Compromise

They say that a relationship is a 50/50 partnership, and you each give 50 percent to the relationship. This isn't always true; in reality, depending on what's going on in your lives, you may be giving 60 percent, while he's only giving 40 percent. Sometimes maybe you need more support, and he's giving 70 percent and you can only give 30 percent. A good relationship allows for balance and compromise when it is necessary. What are you willing to give? If you expect your partner to give 90 percent all of the time, it's probably not going to work.

Think of yourselves as an elite unit. You want to support your teammate and he should support you as well. Men want to treat their women special, but they want to feel special, too. Men understand that women appreciate attention and like to get pampered, and many men want the same type of treatment but rarely say so.

Learn the little things that make your guy feel special and show him that you appreciate him, too. Take your guy to get a pedicure or give him a home spa treatment. If you both have had a bad day, give him the floor to vent about his latest frustrations. Sharing with your partner isn't always about taking turns venting. It's about letting him know that he has a sympathetic ear from someone who cares. Sometimes you have to put your partner's needs before yours. And it goes both ways!

Don't expect that a man will consistently treat you like a princess without you doing things for him. It could be something as simple as doing something nice for him when he least expects it. Let him know you're committed to making things work and being the support he needs. If it's your turn to give an extra 30 percent, then do it. If your relationship is what you want it to be, then you won't always be the one giving more. He'll step up and give you more effort when you need it as well.

Make Your Relationship Work

Any couple that has been married for years will tell you that it is all about the relationship, not the individual. Couples who make it work usually have some kind of pact, spoken or not, that centers around what really keeps them together.

For instance, having a policy that you will never go to bed angry forces you to find resolution and respect one another, no matter what the issue. Some couples always make it a policy to hold hands while discussing tough topics. Other couples have communication helpers such as a cooling-off period before they speak to one another if they're mad. Another idea is to each write out feelings in a notebook, communicating through writing until the heat from an argument subsides.

These ideas for showing love and support will make your relationship last. Be communicative and ensure that your partner knows how to be the same with you. In many cases, a woman will expect that a man should simply know how she feels. Don't make that mistake: *Tell him* how you feel. The more you share with one another, the more you will know what you both need. Establish guidelines that will help you get through the tough times. The more you plan how to deal with the grenades, the more you will avoid having one thrown your way.

Make It Happen!

Share these tips with your partner to help your relationship prosper:

- **Communicate!** If you don't say how you feel, how will your partner truly know what's going on? Be open and share.

- **Treat your partner like a colleague.** Sometimes you're nicer to your co-workers than your significant other. Give your partner the same respect, and communicate with him in a respectful and sane manner.

- **Leave unrelated issues at the door.** If you've had a bad day, keep the outside influences and attitudes away from your relationship. If you need some time to regroup before you interact with your mate, say so. He'll respect you more for asking for a moment than getting into an argument later.

- **Be selfless.** Realize that it's not always all about you. This is where compromise comes in. Put your partner first when he needs support and understanding.

- **Make your relationship all it can be.** Your relationship can be whatever you want it to be. Share with one another what type of relationship you both want now and in the future years to come.

You've taken quite a journey, from improving yourself, finding someone to date, to cultivating that dating experience into a solid and promising relationship. The skills you learned along the way will enhance your well-being so you can function positively and supportively in your new relationship. You and your partner have the tools to establish and maintain the kind of relationship you've always wanted. Continuing to contribute to your own happiness will keep you and your loved one on the right path.

A

Action Plan

Dating Services

Dating services range from individual matchmaking assistance to companies that provide search tools for you to personally find the mate you're looking for. Prices can range from a nominal monthly charge to large flat fees for a pre-arranged number of setups.

Matchmaking services that provide consultative or hands-on assistance are more specialized. They get more details about you through extensive interviews or surveys and introduce you to men who match your needs. These services are more thorough but can be more expensive:

♡ **Matchmaker International**
1-800-772-8818
www.matchmakerintl.com

This service interviews its clients to find out more about them—their interests, background, preferences, and the type of people they would enjoy meeting. Clients fill out a number of questionnaires, which the service uses to match members to other compatible members. The service provides its clients with a set number of matches and the client decides which matches translate into dates.

♡ **Kelleher & Associates**
310-271-6500
www.kelleher-associates.com/about.htm

Kelleher & Associates is a worldwide matchmaking service with offices in San Francisco, Los Angeles, and New York. The service builds its client base working with white-collar professionals, and Kelleher agents create a close rapport with each of their clients to help them find the type of long-term relationship they are looking for. The service sets up matches for the client, and the client decides which matches he or she would like to pursue.

♡ **The Right One**
1-800-818-DATE
www.therightone.com

This is a membership-based service that offers its clients access to a matchmaking database. The Right One uses various learning tools, detailed questionnaires, and a specialized matching system to find the right person for its clients. The service matches the client with a number of prospects and the client decides which to pursue as dates. This service also does a security screening of all clients.

♡ **It's Just Lunch**

212-750-8899

www.itsjustlunch.com

It's Just Lunch is a matching service that sets up one-on-one dates for its clients. Clients have an interview to determine their interests, and dates are set up for lunch or drinks after work based on a preferred list of restaurants.

♡ **Table for Six**

1-888-640-4646

www.tableforsix.com

(Note: Available in Northern California only.) This service matches three men and three women according to their interests, ages, and lifestyles on a dinner date. Clients are free to interact and pursue whom they would like to meet individually at their convenience. In addition, Table for Six offers singles events and activities like weekend trips to Las Vegas, skiing at Lake Tahoe, sporting events, wine country tours, private dinner parties, hiking, speed dating, and international travel.

Some services can be much less expensive (or even nonprofit–based), but you will have to do more of the legwork. Some of these include the following:

♡ **Great Expectations**

www.ge-dating.com

415-321-1900

Great Expectations helps its clients meet other singles by obtaining a profile of what they're looking for and guiding them through videos, photos, and personal profiles. All members are prescreened and prequalified.

♡ **True Love Matching Service**

206-782-4883

www.matchingservice.org

True Love Matching Service is a service that matches clients focused on marriage through religious compatibility. True Love provides educational programs and seminars to assist its members in their search. There are no annual membership fees or dues for the service, but some additional programs and events require a fee.

Internet Dating

Internet dating isn't nearly as scary as it used to be. Generally, online dating sites are less expensive than traditional dating services.

Online sites vary in look and usage—some are easier to navigate than others. Some require a usage fee and others require a membership-based fee to join. Some charge for all online activity, whereas others allow the user to view member profiles and then charge when the user wants to contact a member. Here are just a few:

♡ **www.yahoo.com**   Yahoo! Personals allow users to build a profile and post pictures of themselves. Members can view other members, send a nonpersonalized note to show interest, or e-mail members directly.

♡ **www.match.com**   Match.com is one of the oldest and largest dating services online and has three million singles in its database. Match.com matches members on criteria including age, location, and physical attributes, as well as various personality options. Match.com provides options to save searches and gives weekly notifications containing the most up-to-date search results. Paying members can send as much e-mail to as many members as they like. All members can respond to e-mails from other members, but paying members must initiate the contact.

♡ **www.eharmony.com**   eHarmony is an online dating service for those seeking a more serious relationship. The site uses a matching system based on years of relationship research. Along with a matching system, the site provides guidance, advice, and a structured process for getting to know other members. eHarmony also provides books, tapes, and interactive forums on relationships. The matching process takes a deeper look at a person's beliefs and values rather than simple likes and dislikes. This site is more expensive than traditional online dating services, but it does offer more for serious relationship seekers.

♡ **www.lavalife.com** Lavalife is a global online dating service that has three sites in one service. Members can search through an online database of personal ads for dating, relationships, and casual intimate encounters. There is no charge to post an ad or receive responses.

♡ **www.americansingles.com** American Singles is a global online dating community that provides member profiles to view, as well as online member matching and e-mail functions.

♡ **www.date.com** This online dating site provides photo personals, member profiles, singles events, and dating advice.

♡ **www.matchmaker.com** Matchmaker.com offers free posting of profiles and e-mailing services to members. Members fill out a questionnaire to find the match they are seeking. This site also offers matching by location, interest, or special interest group.

♡ **www.imatchup.com** iMatchup members engage with photo profiles and ratings, live online chat, horoscope matching, targeted search and match capabilities, and e-mail and profile management. There are also feature member contests and promotions with prizes.

♡ **www.dreammates.com** DreamMates offers three dating communities—dating, romance, and intimate— to help singles meet online. Members can post photos and profiles, play games, and express interest to other members for free.

♡ **www.udate.com** A free online service that has thousands of singles to view, all with in-depth photo profiles. UDate offers free registration, which allows users to search the UDate database. Paying members can send e-mail to other members or use the online messaging system. The site also offers a matching feature that automatically searches for other compatible members. Members can prevent members in certain groups from seeing their profile.

♡ **www.matchdoctor.com** MatchDoctor is a free online service where members can perform searches by age, location, personal habits, physical attributes, and religion. Members can also browse by state or search for a particular screen name. Members can post up to five photos.

♡ **www.metrodate.com** Metrodate.com allows members to search profiles with personal messages, photos, videos, and voice messages. Membership is free and members can create their profile, visit the chat rooms and message boards, and view dating tips.

♡ **www.letsmeetup.com** This online service offers photo and video personals.

♡ **www.bigchurch.com**   Big Church provides online dating for people sharing the same religious faith. The site offers free membership, Scripture passages, and an online magazine.

♡ **www.jewishmatchmaker.com**   Jewish Matchmaker connects like-minded Jewish singles online by matching age, lifestyle, and personal goals. The site offers viewing of photo profiles, chat rooms, rabbi advice, and Jewish travel packages.

♡ **www.ebonyconnect.com**   EbonyConnect.com is an online community for meeting African American singles in order to develop friendships and relationships.

Internet Friend/Network Sites
Other ways to connect online include:

♡ **www.friendster.com**   Friendster is an online community that connects people through networks of friends.

♡ **www.citysearch.com**   Citysearch is a leading local search service providing up-to-date information on businesses, from restaurants and retail to travel and professional services.

♡ **www.blackplanet.com**   BlackPlanet.com, an online resource to help African Americans meet other African Americans, has a forum for discussion and provides information that reflects black culture and perspectives.

♡ **www.asiafriendfinder.com** Asia Friendfinder is a dating and community site designed for Asian Americans to meet friends and find serious relationships.

♡ **www.asianavenue.com** AsianAvenue.com is a site for Asian Americans to meet other Asian Americans in their community, express themselves, and find information that reflects Asian culture.

♡ **www.migente.com** MiGente.com reflects Latino perspectives in an online community. This site offers dating profiles, job searches, games, clubs, and chat.

♡ **muybueno.net** Muybueno.net is a website designed to inform and unite the Latino community online and offline. This site promotes education, volunteerism, culture, and business within the community. It also offers mixers, seminars, calendars, and business and services directories.

♡ **club10.com** Club10 is an online site that matches singles between the ages of 21 and 65. The site offers search functions, activities, gatherings across the country, social events, and annual excursions.

Single's Event Calendar

Singles activities are not limited to online dating or the bar scene. See what these sites have to offer you for some fun singles activities in your area. Within these national sites, you can search for your city.

www.matchlive.com

www.singlesonthego.com

www.citysidewalk.com

www.clubzone.com

www.americansocial.com

www.solosingles.com

www.craigslist.com

Here are some sites specific to certain cities:

Chicago—www.singleadvantage.com

New York—www.datinginnewyork.com

Los Angeles—www.lacupid.com

San Francisco—www.serendipity-sf.com

Atlanta—www.atlantasingles.com

Dallas—www.singleindallas.com

Miami—www.miamisinglesonline.com

Washington, D.C.—www.pearz-washington-dc-personals.com

Speed Dating

Speed dating is a great way to meet a lot of new people in a short amount of time. Speed dating sessions usually involve some type of mixer activity before or after the dates to help people interact. Here are just a few speed-dating services:

♡ **www.8minutedating.com**   8minuteDating provides events where members have eight one-on-one dates that last eight minutes each. If both parties are interested in meeting again, they can share contact information to set up another date.

♡ **hurrydate.com**   HurryDate brings members together in a bar setting to have up to 25 dates in one night. Hurry Date caters these events by age and interests.

♡ **www.minidates.com**   Mini Dates sets up members for eight-minute conversations only with those in whom they are interested.

♡ **www.pre-dating.com**   Pre-Dating holds speed-dating events for professional singles based on location and special interest.

♡ **www.3minutedating.com**   Speed dates are set up for members based on age and location. Each date lasts three minutes, and interested participants can exchange contact information.

Volunteer Organizations

Volunteering will help you meet new people and give you the opportunity to give back to your community or the world. Here are some sites of interest:

♡ **www.volunteermatch.org**   VolunteerMatch is a non-profit organization that helps everyone find a great place to volunteer. The site offers a variety of online services to support a community of volunteers and business leaders committed to civic engagement.

♡ **www.helpyourcommunity.org**   This site helps volunteers get involved in various public service campaigns.

♡ **www.unitedway.org**   United Way offers approximately 1,400 community-based United Way organizations that members can volunteer with.

♡ **www.habitat.org**   Habitat for Humanity invites people to work together to eliminate substandard housing worldwide. Habitat offers opportunities to work in many different areas, such as resource development, communications, finance, administration, human resources, operations, programs, information systems, internal audit, legal, and strategic planning.

♡ **www.charityfocus.org/action**   CharityFocus is a volunteer-run nonprofit organization to empower nonprofits with web-based technological solutions. Charity-Focus volunteers help nonprofits to better serve their beneficiaries.

♡ **www.coachart.com**   CoachArt is a nonprofit organization that assists children with life-threatening illnesses by providing free personal lessons in the arts and athletics. CoachArt allows professionals to donate lessons to seriously ill children right in their own neighborhood.

Hobbies and Interest Groups

Meeting with people who have the same interests as you is a great way to expand your singles network. Here are some ideas to help you find people with like interests in your area:

♡ **http://groups.yahoo.com**   Yahoo.com has a variety of groups to choose from. Discuss sports, health, current events, and more with others. Share photos and files, and plan and attend events.

♡ **www.networkingforprofessionals.com**   (Note: Available in New York only.) This professional networking database identifies networking events and business networking groups.

♡ **www.minorityprofessionalnetwork.com**   This site offers a nationwide professional event calendar, business resources, and networking opportunities.

♡ **www.toastmasters.org**   Toastmasters helps its members improve their communication skills. Members lose their fear of public speaking and learn skills to help build their confidence interacting in groups.

Looking for more ideas? Contact the following places for more opportunities in your neighborhood:

♡ Museums

♡ Theater or arts organizations

♡ Chamber of commerce

♡ Community center

♡ City or community newspaper

♡ Charity organizations

♡ Hospitals

♡ City ambassador program

Adventure Dating

Dating is no longer an inside activity! Check out these sites to help you meet active people who want to meet you:

♡ **www.outsidebyside.com** OutSidebySide.com is a site that connects people who enjoy the outdoors and want to meet others with similar interests. Members can make new friends, establish relationships, or obtain "training buddies" through this service.

♡ **www.learningescapes.com** Learning Escapes is a recreational club for the Washington, D.C., metropolitan area. The club offers events for singles such as hiking, photography, and sports and cultural excursions. (Note: Available in Washington, D.C. only)

♡ **www.sierraclub.org** The Sierra Club encourages people to get together to support and protect the environment. Each chapter has various volunteer efforts and outdoor and social activities.

♡ **www.fitkiss.com**   Fitkiss is a dating site for fitness and active friends to meet online.

♡ **www.singlescruise.com** SinglesCruise.com invites single women and men to vacation on cruises geared to singles. Members meet other singles to tour to locations worldwide.

♡ **www.cruisingforlove.com** This site focuses on singles cruises and travel for single adults. Tours go to Caribbean, Mexican, and European destinations.

♡ **www.trekamerica.com** TrekAmerica is an experienced small-group adventure travel operator that caters traveling to singles or small groups. Travel locations include adventures to national parks, tropical beaches, and indigenous civilizations.